METAPHORS

A REVERSE LOVE STORY

VOL. 1

~~Dear Tillman~~
My good friend Merle
says you may find this of
interest (esp. p. 152). Enjoy.
Steve

STEVEN McMANN

Author's Family Room and Upstairs Library

Author's Mother as a Child
"A life dedicated to her children, Jesus, and education"

Published by
Halfcourt Press
conceptsunlimited@estreet.com

Design:
Concepts Unlimited
www.ConceptsUnlimitedInc.com

ISBN-13: 978-0-69223-315-3 (pbk)
ISBN-10: 0692233156

14 15 16 17 18   0 9 8 7 6 5 4 3 2 1

First Printing, 2014
Printed in the United States of America

TABLE OF CONTENTS

Late love

Youth can come and go in heated need,
Their love story told at broadband speed.
Older now we find a better way
With slow hands and more verbal play.
We touch and talk in metaphor,
Finding late love better than before.

METAPHORS:
A REVERSE LOVE STORY

Metaphor: a figure of speech in which a word or phrase literally denoting one kind of object or idea is used in place of another to suggest a likeness or analogy between them (as in "drowning in money").
—Merriam-Webster Dictionary

INTRODUCTION

i awake this morning from a deep sleep with my arms around a naked woman. We are spooned together, my front into her back, fused together in sensual awakening, and I realize this is not a dream. I start to recall bits and pieces of our touching and talking from a similar position during the early morning hours. Not a dream, but it feels like one, as I have not had a naked woman in my bed for years, and not had any sexual contact for almost ten years. I had thought that part of my life was over, and had adjusted to my sexless life with resignation, and it was a fine life, thank you, since I am sixty-seven years old, after all. After all what? And who is this woman moving her backside closer into me this morning? And who am I? I'll tell more of my story later, and ask her to tell hers too, but for now all you need to know is that I awake in wonder at how my life is turning around with this late love.

I am worried that this wonderful woman will jettison me when the reality of our fourteen-year age gap hits her full force, and I tell her so.

"Get real, Steve," Liz immediately responds, "If I wanted to jettison you, there are a hundred other reasons to do so."

"Oh, really?" I reply, "I can only think of seventeen, and I have known myself for a lifetime." Later, still attempting to deflect, "At fifty-three, you're no spring chicken yourself, you know."

Variations on her wise-ass remark will henceforth lighten our discussion of the age gap, and be a source of amusement to our

3

friends. My friend, Paul, will introduce himself to her as "102," meaning, of course, that she can add him to the list of reasons she could dump me if she wanted. She decides to call him 102, later shortened to 02, thus giving new and longer life to the joke.

We think of it as our reverse love story, because most people focus on young love almost to the exclusion of late love. *Love Story* by Erich Segal is one of our generation's most famous versions of young love, especially after Erich's bestseller turned to the big screen. I can call Erich by his first name, as he was my Shakespeare tutor at Harvard College, a promising classical scholar laboring over obscure academic publications before his simple story of young love catapulted him to fame and fortune. Erich cultivated a friendship with me as a fellow athlete, he a long distance runner and I a basketball jock. Liz also considers herself a jock, lettering in three sports at Harvard (ice hockey, lacrosse and crew), although we would not meet until almost a lifetime later. So as we marvel at how good, and even better, our sex life and time together is at this late stage of life, and how different our lives and perceptions have been, we decide to tell our story in alternate chapters of this book.

bagman

A wild look from wrinkled face
Babbling nonsense to whomever
Inhabits his inner space
The old Chinese bagman never
Meant us any kind of offense
But it made no difference
Since we awkwardly inched away
As from leper in former day.
Hair all faded white and thin
Like the suit he skeletoned in.
Yet hint of sparkle in his eye
Like a lone star in twilight sky
And smile shy to dignify
Discards he couldn't afford to buy.
We watched him reach to disinter
Beer cans from debris in dumpster
Sipping from one not quite empty
Oblivious to our company.
Puffed on a half-lit cigarette
For the last smoke left in it yet.
Slim silhouette against sunset
He pulled from inside vest pocket
And soft across harmonica blew
A happy tune we all once knew
Drawing us from our present place
Briefly into his inner space.
Then nodded as if to say good day,
Picked up his bag, and walked away.

Chapter 1
"NOT LOOKING FOR ANYONE OR ANYTHING"

i met Liz about ten years ago at a Harvard Club bowling event that she had organized at an athletic club in downtown Boulder, Colorado. At the time, Pam, my main squeeze for twelve years and I had amicably agreed to go separate ways, and once again I was unattached and looking for female companionship. Although Liz is not beautiful in the Barbie doll or movie star way, and you would not pick her out of a police lineup as a "hottie," I was immediately attracted to her. She has an interesting face framed by glasses and a knockout smile. She wears almost no make-up. She dresses in an understated way that somewhat disguises her substantial breasts and strong athletic frame, and I find this attractive in several ways. I am repulsed by high maintenance, vacuous women (Barbies) who spend a lot of time and money to project an attractive appearance to the world. As a six foot six man now about forty pounds over his two hundred ten college playing weight, I am attracted to full-bodied women built like Sophia Loren or Silver Pansy (book cover), while skinny women with toothpick legs are a definite turn-off. I can tell that Liz is smart and fun by the witty remarks that crack me up as we bowl surprisingly badly considering our athletic propensities. Later I will tell you about her apt bowling ball metaphor, but for now all you need to know is that she is married, and therefore unavailable.

After Pam, my live-in girlfriend for twelve years, torpedoes my 'living apart together' dream by marriage to a cowboy, I continue to go to Harvard Club events over the next ten years with the ulterior motive of meeting a compatible woman, but always am disappointed and wish I had not bothered. In fact, over those ten years I almost always get bored with perfectly fine women on occasional dates, and conclude that I would rather stay at home by the fireplace with a good book than engage in social activities. And then I do so, becoming somewhat reclusive, but finding that a monastic lifestyle seems suited to me. I resign myself to a sexless single life, but am concerned that it may not be a matter of choice any longer when one day I am aroused by an erotic movie on TV and go upstairs to my bedroom to masturbate, and discover that by the time I reach the bed, I had lost interest and would rather read a book. This happens several times over the next few months, and I begin to worry that my abstinence is no longer a matter of choice. Use it, or lose it. So several times I try to spank the monkey to orgasm. When I come, it is with little pleasure. I am alarmed that my equipment no longer seems to be in working order. I discover a possible explanation on my sixty-fifth birthday at a physical examination recommended by my new Medicare brochure. The doc tells me I have atrial fibrillation, and later tests confirm unfixable Afib. Afib, my cardiologist explains, means that my arrhythmic heart pumps about twenty percent less blood and oxygen to my extremities, and therefore, I conclude, to both of my male brains.

So my social skills, never that great to begin with, are rusty and my equipment problematic when at a Harvard Club event I learn that Liz has been divorced for almost two years. She lives in a big house in Boulder with her two children and a dog.

As President of the local Harvard Club, Liz is organizing an event — a Palestinian speaker on radical Islam invited by a Boulder Jewish organization. When I call-in my acceptance, Liz invites me to a small dinner party she is hosting beforehand, and I learn that, like me, she "is not looking for anyone or anything." But that is about to change, for both of us, since every time we get together, everything; our first hug, first kiss, first sleepover; seems so easy and natural and fun. Here are a few examples to give you a sense of how my life (Our lives? But she can tell her "I" story separately before it merges into a "we" story.) has changed. I will start by inserting the Wish List that I sent to Liz during an early e-mail exchange.

Dear Liz,

Our various conversations have forced me to consider what I am looking for in a relationship. This Relationship Wish List (RWL) may seem simplistic and even naive, but until we connected recently, I was not looking for a relationship at all. "Not looking for anyone or anything," as you so succinctly put it. This just-conceived list is also self-centered, but it helps me prioritize and clarify, so here goes.

First and foremost, a good woman whose need for independence is as strong as my own so both have substantial personal freedom (but not sexual freedom) within the relationship.

Second, a good woman who loves to hug, touch and cuddle through the night as much as I do.

Third, a good woman who loves to share intimate thoughts and feelings as well as intellectual discussion.

Fourth, a good woman to go to movies, parties, sports and other activities that can be awkward as a single.

Fifth, a good woman to join me for tennis, biking, swimming or even hoops.

Sixth, a good woman who enjoys having sex with me.

Explanation for above prioritization:

Number 1: Without a substantial degree of independence and personal space, it seems to me that intimate relationships come with a lot of questionable trade-offs, which is probably why I have never married.

Number 6 was number one thirty years ago when my hormones were still raging and my body still muscular and attractive. Now that I am a 67 year-old man with love handles, bull legs(!), a paunch and a 20 percent energy-depleting Afib heart, Number 6 would be nice if it is mutually enjoyable, but dispensable if not. I have lived a reasonably happy life for several years without a sexual relationship, and could do so again if necessary.

Number 3 probably would be number 1 or 2 for most people, but what I miss most in a relationship is sleeping throughout the night with my arms around a woman. I can always find the intellectual and emotional stimulation of number 3 from my love of reading, but a good book cannot take the place of the warm and loving body of a good woman.

I put number 4 ahead of number 5 because I can always find some guy to participate in number 5 activities, but a woman is essential for number 4 activities.

I would be happy to realize any one of the six objectives on this wish list, very happy with a combination of the six and blessed beyond belief for all six. It may be presumptuous, but I think we will share at least one of these objectives, and there is even a chance of all six with you, so I hope that I will be able to meet one or more of your relationship objectives, whether you choose to put them in writing or not. I offer this list in the hope that it will have some value for further discussion, but let me know if you think it is counterproductive overkill.

Perhaps the entire list could be summarized in the repeated as-sumption of "a good woman," but of course that is too vague to be helpful. Similarly, number 2 could be summarized as Hugs! So I really like your recent "Hugs!" sign-off to me and suggest that it should be our default sign-off on all communication (if you agree, of course). Hugs!
Steve

Yes, I know that sharing my Relationship Wish List with Liz will strike most observers as unwise. Making a Wish List is not uncommon. My college friends and I would often compare Wish Lists. They help to focus on what you seek in a partner and help prioritize the qualities that make the list. Sharing your Wish List with a potential mate, however, is almost unheard of. Sure, sharing certainly has potential to create problems, but at my age I don't have time to play the usual games. I think this kind of open and honest disclosure of wishes can distinguish our late love from the nonverbal miscommunications of young love.

Placing sex as number six is not a ploy, but reality, probably for the Afib reasons explained earlier. I know I can live without sex, but miss the number 2 spooning and related companionship; if it can be had without impinging too much on my all-important number 1, freedom. I reluctantly admit to myself that I have become increasingly lonely over the years, and really miss the touching and talking of a good relationship, and "touch and talk" ("TNT") becomes shorthand for our relationship as Liz and I do both extensively throughout the ensuing days and nights. Number six, sex, highlights the first of the many different ways Liz and I perceive the same facts or events since she thinks the wording is very self-centered (focusing on Me and what I want). This surprises me because I was careful to word number six to emphasize mutuality. Liz responds to my Relationship Wish List one month later.

So, Steve...

I'm re-reading this with fresh eyes.

First, are you getting enough personal freedom? Am I impinging at all?

Second, I would venture that I'm doing OK with this. OK???? Terrifically. I love waking up with you, talking about big things and little without concern about any nakedness (literal or figurative).

Third, uh, is there anything I haven't told you? Surely there is, and it will surface. What would you say if I indicated that I wanted your mind more than your body?

Fourth, well we went to the movies once. You attended a dinner party, once, with me. I have you on the hook for one lax game and the finale of the NCAA tournament. Seems like #6 has surpassed #4 for the time being. Need I apologize?

Fifth, am game.

Sixth, am a player.

I look forward to exploring number 1, just so I understand the parameters.

Hugs,

Liz

I was hoping for a corresponding Relationship Wish List (RWL) from Liz, summarizing her goals and prioritizing them. I start to compose what I think is probably her RWL in my head, and conclude that she is looking for a traditional marriage within which to raise her two children. After all, Liz several times has stated that her children are her number one priority, and perhaps Liz sees our alternative relationship as LATs (Living Apart Together) as undercutting that goal. The more I think about it the more I'm sure that Liz's number one goal is marriage.

So this thought is keeping me up through the middle of the night and half the morning, underscoring my RWL preoccupation with my number one priority of freedom and independence. We'll call it number one because, like the first person tense in which this story is written, it also is symbolic of my self-centered needs being the highest priority. Which probably is the main reason I have never married. Like Oliver's admission in the first paragraph of Erich Segal's *Love Story* that he always has to be number one, I admit that I always have to be number one. The only time that I was disciplined for bad behavior in high school was when I refused to play second-chair coronet to the more accomplished first-chair coronet. I was told that I could not play the melody, but I didn't really care much because I would be playing basketball. I knew that while the band was playing in the orchestra pit, I would be number one — five steps above on the hardwood. So I am self-centered and competitive and marriage is the ultimate test of compromise and cooperation.

The assumed RWL thus reflects my fear that Liz's number one goal of providing for and protecting her children may be the same as most single women: marriage. Some may argue that the male goal of independence does not conflict with the female goal of marriage, and that true independence can only be achieved within marriage. I am willing to explore the concept with Liz, but I don't believe it. But does Liz believe it? Reflection on our recent touch and talk convinces me now that she does. You can call me stupid or naïve or whatever for even putting these fears into writing at this point in our relationship. I don't care. I want to be open and honest with Liz, especially on this most important matter. If marriage is her goal, then we should part ways now before we both get hurt due to this fundamental misunderstanding.

This is a book about love — late love. Some would argue that love is defined by voluntarily giving up freedom and forgoing the "I" to achieve the "we" that marriage represents. I don't believe this either. In fact I am not sure I believe in love — at least the way most people define it. I also don't believe in God — at least the way most people define it — but that is a subject for another time. So my immediate goal is to provoke Liz to talk about this marriage issue and hopefully to explain her wish list priorities, even if not in writing. Liz's e-mail in response to my wish list is thoughtful, but you may have noticed that she did not address the marriage issue. We need to talk some more. Preferably talk and touch some more.

There probably are a hundred other reasons why I have never married. The most common explanation I hear from others is that I am looking for the perfect woman, implying of course that I am too picky. To deflect, I usually reply, "You are wrong. I have found the perfect woman many times. The problem is that they all were looking for the perfect man."

Actually, the problem is the assumption that marriage is the ultimate goal of any healthy relationship, and that any relationship not headed in that direction is somehow diminished and not worth pursuing. This assumption is so universally shared that I hesitate to become involved with another woman for fear of misleading her about my intentions. I agree that marriage makes sense when there are children to protect, but I have never felt the need to produce offspring, in part because my siblings are busy populating the world. The assumption of marriage as goal is so universal that women tend to see anyone who does not share it as a commitment phobe rather than a freedomphile, a concept so foreign that my computer underlines it in red as a word not found in the dictionary. I can commit to a monogamous relationship, but not to marriage. I place a high value on my independence and freedom, and thus the rationale for number one on my wish list. Love does not need marriage to prosper, in fact often hinders. The argument has been made better elsewhere as in the book *Not Love* by L. Kipnis. So the "perfect woman" for me would know that love and commitment can be found outside of marriage.

Of course there is no such thing as the perfect woman or perfect man. Everyone has their good and bad points, their strengths and weaknesses. It is what makes us human. And no reasonable person expects to find the perfect mate. But most of the women I have shared my life with have been wonderful in different ways, and convince me that women in general are stronger than men in the nonphysical ways that really matter. They tend to be more sensitive, more forgiving, more cooperative, more giving, more of almost everything, than I and my male counterparts who I am sorry to say tend to be rather self-centered and competitive like me. So I tend to put women on a pedestal as if all were as good and strong as my mother, and the question is whether this provides the basis for a healthy relationship.

So when I meet Liz I am hopeful that there will be an overlap of a few wishes, and am astonished that she seems to meet all of them. In fact, Liz not only meets all six wishes on my original Relationship Wish List, but several others that expand the list as follows:

Seventh, a good woman who is financially independent. Since Liz had told me early in our relationship that an important priority for her was finding a job, I assumed that her financial situation after the divorce was precarious. A number of misunderstandings followed from this assumption. For example, in helping Liz find a rental and later a house, I focused on affordable alternatives. Later she disclosed that her trust fund was several million dollars, and she could afford an expensive house even after paying private tuition for her children. Liz indeed is a rich girl from a blueblood Boston family. She needed a job for self-esteem, not to pay the rent and put bread on the table. My main concern was that I didn't want a woman who would be dependent upon me financially, and therefore potentially undermine the financial independence I had achieved and valued so much. Beyond that, I didn't care how much money she had, or how she spent it. Actually, she spent relatively little on herself, but an outrageous amount on her children. Separate bank accounts were ideal, and removed a major cause of discord among couples (finances being one of the most common causes of conflict and divorce among couples).

Eighth, a good woman who prefers a separate house. In addition to providing the psychological space needed for independence, a separate house was physically important since my big box was already full of material possessions. As Liz so succinctly put it upon first seeing my house, "If I moved into your house, there wouldn't be room for my tennis racquet." An exaggeration of course since there is always room in my house for another book or two, but not much else. In fact Liz has two storage lockers full of inherited furniture and other possessions in addition to her possessions from her big "divorce house." Liz needs her own house for her own possessions, and in which to raise her children. Alternatively, and not a realistic possibility, if I moved into Liz's upscale house, there wouldn't be room for my basketball. Living Apart Together (LAT), a new trend with many couples, seemed ideal. Living close, but apart, guaranteed close comfort as well as substantial independence.

Ninth, a good woman who is not a passive lover. As will be obvious in Chapter four, Liz is not a passive lover. She takes the initiative much of the time, and usually is open about what she likes and dislikes. I on the other hand tend to be a passive lover, very sensitive about making unwanted advances (one of the worst male offenses in my view). Liz does not play the "run until she catches me" game. She seems open, honest and direct in initiating many sexual pleasures. There must be a God!

So nine for nine is not only winning the lottery, but a national power-ball lottery. For me Liz is the complete package, "the package," or simply "pack." Of course this begs the question of how much of my wish list overlaps with hers, but she is smart enough or careful enough not to be that obvious. But I hope that as a recently divorced woman she has no illusions about marriage, and is not ready to take that route again.

When we touch and talk ("TNT") again she is amused at my speculation about her marriage/father goals saying they are a figment of my runaway imagination. Her children already have a father, she says, and she would not want me to attempt to substitute for him. More important, she is still recovering from the trauma of her marriage and divorce, and re-marriage is not even on her radar. Unburdened of this fear, I find Liz even more attractive than before. I do not have to feel guilty about wasting her time. We can move forward in our relationship if she wants. Of course now the focus becomes number six and my doubts pertaining to my equipment. But I am more than willing to move forward if she is.

march madness

with apologies to ee cummings

Play ball, said he
That's all? asked she.

Game's on, said he.
UConn's big, said she.

I've got Duke, said he.
Coach's got toupee? asked she.

Illegal pick! yelled he.
Hairy armpits, said she.

Ref's a dick, screamed he.
Looks so small, sighed she.

Double dribble, cried he.
Long shorts, no sleeves, said she.

Great shot, cried he.
He's hot, said she.

Tar Heels rock, said he.
Just jumping jocks, joked she.

Flagrant foul, yelled he.
Why the scowl? asked she.

One and done, groaned he.
Skinny legs, said she.

Hit the glass, yelled he.
Nice ass, sighed she.

V.C.U., cheered he.
I need you, gasped she.

Go Bull Dogs, said he.
They're so cute, said she.

Hold them, begged he.
I'd like to, said she.

No tip-in, screamed he
Tip in me, thought she.

KEN TUCK EE! yelled he.
Please...hold me, moaned
she.

Finals next week, said he.
April madness? asked she.

Chapter 2
REVERSE LOVE STORY

in my Wish List, I outlined what I believed was improbable and emphasized that I would be happy if I could find just a few of my six wishes in a woman. I soon realized that with Liz I had won the lottery again as she embodied all six and more. Liz is the Complete Package. So I nicknamed her "my Package," later shortened to "Packer," "Pack" and then variations like "D-Pack" as a double entendre on her defensive specialty in sports and her 36 D-cup bra. This was the start of a special language "we" were developing together as metaphor that we could use in public and private without embarrassment. It took the edge off the more vulgar words like "pussy" and "prick" when we substituted "Bermuda" and "Laz" for vagina and penis.

Relationship Wish List
On my wish list sex was six,
Freedom one, and cuddle two.
Then smarts added to the mix,
And sports at five important too.
So no Barbie doll for me.
Then I won the lottery
With Liz of three-letter fame
Plus tennis lets us cross-train
Bringing Laz back from the dead
With tricks she plays with my head.

So number six merges with two,
I score full list, not just a few.
She's the complete package I know
From Bermuda to big D, head to toe,
She seems a perfect DePack
Says our age gap no cause to worry
Given a hundred other reasons to dump me.

Steve, "You know, Liz, our relationship is almost a reverse love story."

Liz, "What do you mean?"

Steve, "Well, in Erich Segal's *Love Story*, the rich Harvard boy falls in love with the poor Radcliffe girl. You are a rich Boston girl falling in love with a poor midwestern boy."

Liz, "Who said I was falling in love? That's another reason I could jettison you. I've always hated the word. It implies and promises too much."

Steve, "Yes, I have always avoided the word because if I say I love you, then you can and probably will say if you love me, then you should x, y and z."

Liz, "I just don't know what it means, or if it's possible."

Steve, "Segal writes about young love. We could write our late love story."

Liz, "Our boomer generation might be interested in late love."

Steve, "Especially if we write it to show the many ways late love can be better than young love."

Liz, "Because it is more mutual?"

Steve, "And more verbal. Like when we talk explicitly about sex."

Liz, "Yes. Our metaphors will soften the story."

Steve, "Like Bermuda."

Liz, "Like Laz."

Steve, "In place of `Love means never having to say you're sorry,' our reverse catchphrase can be `Love means always giving the benefit of the doubt.' "

Liz, "I like it. You know, writing about reverse love could be fun."

Steve, "We need to be careful about our metaphors. Reverse love sounds like anal sex."

Liz, "You have a problem with that?"

Steve, "No, full speed ahead."

Liz, "We're going to be rich and famous when the book is a best seller."

Steve, "The publishers will fight each other to get us to sign with them."

Liz, "We'll negotiate a tough deal for the movie rights."

Steve, "And the residuals, like rubber Bermudas and Lazes."

Liz, "We will be rich beyond our dreams, but not famous like Segal."

Steve, "Why not?"

Liz, "Think about it. Even with metaphors, if we write as explicitly as we talk and act, it will be X rated. And my family can't know."

Steve, "We will have to use pseudonyms so no one will be able to connect us to the book."

Liz, "So no book tours."

Steve, "No Jon Stewart interviews."

Liz, "Not even Colbert?"

Steve, "Not even Colbert."

Liz, "I don't really need the fame. We can live with just the riches."

Steve, "Life is full of trade-offs."

the gender gap

A cosmic joke
God's master stroke
Setting the trap
Called gender gap.

Divine ad-lib
From Adam's rib
Left handicap
Called gender gap.

Eve had her pick
Of just one chap
A cosmic trick
That gender gap.

With man as mate
God sealed Eve's fate
Sent her a chap
With gender gap.

Eve played the trick
Gave man a kick
In gender gap
That tender trap.

The gender gap
Is not complex
She wants more love
And he more sex.

Yet that same gap
Has grown so wide
It's hard to bridge
From either side.

Lovers have found
No way around
The gender trap
That tender gap.

Love's always been
A tender trap
When you fall in
The gender gap.

The gender gap
Such wide divide
Most love gets trapped
Deep down inside.

The gender gap
Now so complex
It's hard to bridge
By either sex.

The gender gap
Has grown so wide
You need a map
To find each side.

Love is the map
You need to bridge

The gender gap
From ridge to ridge.

Thus love provides
Bridge cross divides
That handicap
The gender gap.

This love's so good
All couples should
Now cheer and clap
For gender gap.

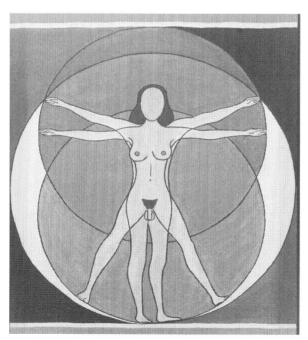

"Gender Gap" by Author

Chapter 3
BLACK BRA

the gender gap crashed our party almost before it got started. Like many issues dividing couples, the trigger was sex, even though I had tried to downplay it as number six very low on my Relationship Wish List (RWL). I was astounded that Liz saw the wording as self-centered when I had been careful to draft number six to be mutual (thinking that her list if shared would have something similar: a good man who enjoys having sex with me). I am reminded of Deborah Tannen's fascinating *You Just Don't Understand*, which explores the many ways in which words mean different things to men and women. There you have it: the gender gap (poem 5, pg 22-23) that can quickly morph into the gender trap if a couple is not careful. And careful obviously is not enough as my number six illustrates. Maybe Tannen offers seminars.

Getting the "me" versus "we" issue into our relationship early is helpful. Front and center we can deal with it rather than having it lurking ominously below the surface. Like Oliver Barrett in *Love Story,* my whole life has been focused on "I" and a self-centered and even narcissistic approach to the world. I need to focus more on the "we" rather than my customary "me." The theme of mutuality will run through our entire relationship as Liz and I agree that none of it is worthwhile if not mutual. This is true not only for our sexual exploration, but also for every other aspect of our lives together.

I think Liz is especially sensitive to these gender issues because she resented her Ex's narcissistic alternative. The "Four Steps Behind" metaphor stems from Liz and her children being left four steps behind Jerque Johnson as he pushes forward on his own. This is a good metaphor as it describes an attitude that permeates every aspect of their former marriage. I suffer from the same self-centered illness, but not to the extent Jerque does. I would like to show Liz that I am not like her ex.

As Liz explains, I need to focus more on the "we" rather than the "I" narrative, and this is difficult, given a lifetime of "I" focus, but I am learning — I think. And I like Liz's "we" emphasis since it implies joint ventures and a future together. The most difficult part of the "we" transition for me is in the bedroom where Liz needs to continue to reassure me that male orgasm is not as important as prolonged pleasure in sexual play. This observation probably won't be of interest to those caught up in young or even middle-aged passion, but boomers like us in late love stages may identify with similar experience. Technically, we are both boomers (defined as those born between 1942 and 1964), and I am **not** old enough to be her father. Yet the reality is that our fourteen-year age difference could become an issue. We have put the age difference front and center as a continuing joke based on Liz's smart-ass remark about "a hundred other reasons," but the fourteen-year age difference is still troublesome. I can try to bridge the gender gap, but I cannot do much about the age gap.

The gender gap was highlighted again when Paul sent Liz the Black Bra joke that men have circulated on the Internet for years. Liz reads black bra from a woman's point of view. My, what a difference.

Steve,
    Fair warning: I'm also sending Black Bra to Liz.
Paul

The Black Bra (told by a woman)…

I had lunch with two of my unmarried friends. One is engaged, one is a mistress and I have been married for twenty plus years.

We were chatting about our relationships and decided to amaze our men by greeting them at the door wearing a black bra, stiletto heels and a mask over our eyes. We agreed to meet in a few days to exchange notes.

Here's how it all went.

My engaged friend:

The other night when my boyfriend came over he found me with a black leather bodice, tall stilettos and a mask.

He saw me and said, "You are the woman of my dreams. I love you." Then we made passionate love all night long.

The mistress:

Me too! The other night I met my lover at his office and I was wearing a raincoat, under it only a black bra, heels and a mask over my eyes. When I opened the raincoat he didn't say a word but he started to tremble and we had wild sex all night.

Then I had to share my story:

When my husband came home I was wearing a black bra, black stockings, stilettos and a mask over my eyes.

When he came in the door and saw me he said, "What's for dinner, Batman?"

Liz,

Very funny. "What's for dinner, Batman," is one of the all time great lines — almost as good as "I'll have what she's having."
Steve

Steve,

It's always so interesting to get the perspective from the other side!! I didn't know about the line, so in effect this email circulated among women is a bunch of women whining that when you're married for a long time, you get a snappy verbal quip that illustrates his cleverness rather than the sexual passion that you so dearly crave (illustrated by 1 and 2). She felt rejected and treated like a child.

However, what if one was to look at it differently, or to finish the story. She answers, something to the effect of "it's a new recipe: c'mon and find out; who's hungry for what?" Whatever. In a good relationship the story wouldn't have ended there. It would have been a beginning, because the relationship is safe and both people can ask for what they want.

The 1 and 2 versions are actually; well they are missing a lot too. One night of wild or passionate lovemaking is great, don't get me wrong, and the afterglow is nothing to be ashamed of. I would imagine that being a mistress is more of a fantasy play (for those who aren't) about great sex without constraints, getting a rich sugar daddy, not having to deal with a guy on a day-to-day basis, etc.

Now, Paul, which version does he really want?
Liz

Liz,

Thanks again for joining me for my great nephew's game, and also for the leftovers afterwards. Another enjoyable evening, and this time I left before you had to start hinting about doing so.   Re-reading your perceptive comments about gender different versions and interpretations of Black Bra, I wonder if you might be hearing my various comments about commitment and relationships in the same way (different from the way I intend them), especially because I have a sense of being   inarticulate in elaborating on some of these issues. I was   relieved when you said you also like to hold someone throughout the night regardless of sex, (not to dismiss the special attraction of the latter), and need time to figure some of this out. I hereby promise to stop over-analyzing a relation-ship that has yet to evolve, other than to repeat that I really enjoy your company and look forward to our next time together. My turn to provide the meal. Do you know of any place that would go well with a dose of Darwin?
Steve

Steve,

I've been chastising myself for talking too much and not listening well enough when I'm with you. I really, really appreciate your opening up about Pam. It's all hard to figure out, because someone, either one (of a M/F), will say some-thing and not want to create a burden or share too much for personal reasons, which of course is fine. But then the other one doesn't want to pry into the personal pain, but still is overtly or subliminally collecting data and creating impres-sions.

He calls himself a recluse. He lives in a house with books. He's well educated. He likes to exercise. She doesn't think she's smart, but she's wise. She's got 2 kids, recently divorced. Downsizing from a big house. What's this about supporting the kids???

Liz

senses

Roses I have smelled at sunrise
And heard many a symphony
Seen rainbows over the mountains
And suns set light into the sea
But your warm body one with mine
Has made the greatest sense to me.

afterglow

We in afterglow lay naked
In warm water back-to-womb bed
Yet wrapped in each other's caress
And in moon shrouded darkness
Through open window drifting in
Primal cadence of cricket choir
And light breeze touching soft our skin
Rekindling embers of desire
Thus well dressed in natural attire
We come in such moments to sense
The only things of consequence.

Chapter 4
FIRST TIME

i wake about 7:30 a.m. and think about the discussion Liz and I had about finding an appropriate name for a certain member of mutual interest (my penis). I suggest Lazarus as in `Raising Lazarus from the Dead.' Perhaps just `Laz' for short and `Bermuda' for his counterpart, saying it's no good unless mutual. Liz has talked about her vagina as her Bermuda triangle, emphasizing the mysteries contained and still undiscovered.

Liz calls in response to e-mails and has not read the messages and does so while we talk so I get real time feedback from her. At one point during this intimate conversation I tell Liz that Laz has turned all hard, wet and excited. Liz suggests that I give Laz a good workout today (i.e. masturbate) and I suggest she do the same with Bermuda and also get some extra sleep because she is certainly sleep deprived after a long weekend we had spent together talking and touching, but stopping at second base.

About 1 p.m. I am still thinking about our sensual weekend and Laz is all hot and bothered again. So I go upstairs to follow Liz's suggestion and this time I do not opt for a nap instead. I have a magnificent orgasm and e-mail Liz that I have followed her suggestion and have details upon request. When Liz calls after my swim at Boulder Athletic Club (BAC) she laughs and it is clear she knew exactly what I meant. I say that there is now one very wet paper towel in the wastebasket next to my bed. Then the stunner; Liz says she also took my advice regarding Bermuda and assures me that all her equipment appears to be in working order as well. We laugh at this mutual admission (which seems very bold given our private tendencies) and so another parallel can be added to the mutuality picture (i.e. we are like virgins but without the teenage hang-ups).

This afternoon Liz calls to ask if I still have *The Winslow Boy* DVD. I do and we arrange for her to come by my place to see it tonight. She will arrive about 5 p.m., and says that she will not stay over because she wants to take everything slow so we get to know each other better and so will leave by 9 p.m. I say we have plenty of time, so there is no hurry and I am delighted that she can come by. I say that if it were up to me I would not let her leave, so it is good that she has a plan. I say that I don't have a clue about her sometimes, but am ready to learn and would appreciate her encouragement and discouragement as she thinks appropriate. Somewhere in here we talk about the need for mutuality and I stress that nothing is worth it if not mutual. Then she says that leaving early is hard on her too and I say that this makes me feel so much better. She says, "Yes, I am human and a sexual being, but we need to know each other better." So all is well and will be better about 5 p.m. today. Liz arrives about 5:30 p.m. and so begins one of the best evenings of my life. No kidding, even if unlikely at 67 years of age.

The evening can be divided into parts:
1. Foot massages and hugs and heavy kissing and petting.
2. Watch *The Winslow Boy*.
3. More hugging and kissing on the sofa while listening to Leonard Cohen's *Live in London* CD.
4. Tyson's beef pot roast dinner, with potato salad and a fruit bowl.
5. Back to sofa for even more intense touching, groping and some talking.

What is surprising is how easy our talk and touching is; so natural and uninhibited. At one point after massaging Liz's feet and legs she says, "You are hired." But I hear it as "You are hard," and say, "Yes, for about the last half hour." We laugh at the mistake and she says she doesn't think I will have a problem in that area. We agree again to take it slow, but she is grinding Bermuda hard against my leg and I am grabbing her rear with one hand and the other high on the thigh of her corduroy trousers and she is moaning. She moans also as I blow into and then lick each ear, and I moan when she puts my index finger into her mouth and starts sucking. It feels so good and sensual. I hold her head and I touch her breasts and she slides on top of me and the fit feels very good. Our kisses tonight are passionate, complete with Frenching. I tell her my fantasy about how when she feels comfortable with me I want her to take off all her clothes and lie on her back on the bed with her hands behind her head and then I will softly touch her all over her body, and I mean all over and she must not touch or pull me close to her, but simply lie still and receive the complete attention of my touching. I ask her what she thinks of my fantasy and she says it sounds wonderful, except we might have to have had some sexual contact earlier or she would not be able to stay still.

Later she says that at some point she wants to do the same to me and discover all my sensitive parts. I say she has already made a good start. At one time she accidentally touches an erect Laz and says she will not touch Laz because she doesn't want to tease me and I say I don't mind and she can tease me all she wants because teasing is very underrated. Liz apologies somewhat for all of her grinding on my leg and I say I loved every second of it. I touch her ample breasts underneath her shirt and she lets me, but my touching is soft and over the top of her bra and she pants and says she cannot wait until we have sex, and that may be soon, like perhaps the next time we are together. She asks if her body feels like a twenty-five year old woman and I tell her it feels just fine and we need to forget the fact that we don't have young bodies anymore and I wouldn't trade the pleasure of our touching for young bodies and she agrees. Some things are better with age.

The dinner is natural like the touching. We talk over a meal I prepare that she seems to like and we eat in the dining room in candlelight. In addition to the pot roast and potato salad I have cut fruit dishes of strawberry, apple and banana followed by one piece of Russell Stover dark chocolate for dessert. When we kiss on the sofa later Liz says she can taste the chocolate in my mouth. She also says that I overwhelm her and I say she has overwhelmed me since we met a few weeks ago. We listen to a Leonard Cohen CD and she likes it as much as I do.

The night has gone fast and hot, fun and memorable; and we agree to get together on Friday for free guest day at Boulder Athletic Club for some exercise and then go to the Darwin movie, *Creation*. She leaves about 11:45 p.m. long after her planned 9 p.m. departure. I joke that sometimes plans are overrated and we need to improvise. So ends a memorable day.

It keeps getting better with Liz. Last night and this morning proved the best times yet. Liz comes by my place about 3:30 p.m. A late winter storm is moving through the area. We move to the sofa and start talking and touching and we are heating up fast, so we decide to go for our Boulder Athletic Club free guest day workout as previously agreed so we don't get sidetracked.

In unusual traffic on the way to the athletic club I joke that Liz surely cannot risk going home tonight with all the ice and snow and what a shame that she is probably snowed in at my house for the night. Liz smiles and says, "We'll see," and immediately I am full of hope that Liz indeed will stay over tonight for the first time. I show Liz around BAC and we meet at the basketball court where I give Liz some basic shooting tips like using fingertips rather than palm and putting reverse spin on the ball and using the glass as her friend for higher percentage shooting. She does not have the strength to do so from long range but quickly finds the spot on the backboard for lay-ups from the right and left side. She is thinking about my suggestions and trying to break down each move of the lay-up and other shots. With practice she could be good which is not surprising for an athlete who earned three major letters at Harvard.

I get on the rowing machine and Liz gives me tips on how to maximize my rowing power such as strapping my feet into the machine so they don't come back on the pulling stroke. I go to the stationary bike to spin for ten minutes while Liz stays at the rowing machine, which is twice as hard, but continues for another ten minutes. We meet at the indoor pool where the swim coach has cleared a lane for us upon my request and I swim a lap before Liz joins me. She looks great in her one-piece bathing suit and at the far end of the pool she straddles me with both legs around my back before releasing quickly in embarrassment that other swimmers might notice this provocative position. I joke that no one can see under water or would care anyway. I do my usual side and back strokes in the shared lane while Liz alternates between the crawl and breaststroke. It is not surprising that she is a good swimmer, but she says she has always disliked swimming since seven years old since it is so boring. I agree and tell her I always try to have a problem or something specific to think about to distract me from the boredom of swimming. I tell her about the drop-dead beauty in grade school who taught me how to swim and her comment that I could swim forever using the sidestroke and never get tired.

We stop to talk occasionally during our swim and agree to take a leisurely sauna and whirlpool in our respective locker rooms before meeting upstairs at about 7:30 p.m. So we have been at BAC for three and a half hours of enjoyable exercise and talk.

Back home again in time for the Jon Stewart and Stephen Colbert shows which Liz has never seen since she does not have cable. Stewart is doing a parody of Glen Beck, who Liz has never heard of, but we miss Colbert's parody of the Catholic church because we again are all over each other on the couch. Liz says, "I may regret this in the morning, but let's go upstairs to your bed." I of course am overjoyed with this suggestion and upstairs we remove some of each other's clothing. Soon we are in bed and the rest of our clothing is on the floor. Liz is gorgeous. I tell her later that she does not have the body of a 52 year-old woman.

She obviously likes my compliment. She has the most beautiful full breasts I have ever seen and even better than I had imagined. "And they're real," I say, comparing them to the silicone which is so often on parade at BAC. "And they're yours," Liz says "so go ahead and play with them." I do and she moans in pleasure, which leads to my hands all over, and then in her "Bermuda Triangle," as she cleverly puts it.

Liz is on her back and I kneel between her legs and tell her how beautiful she looks; adding that she cannot know because she does not have the perspective that I do on the "future of the world." My metaphor is not as good as hers but she gets the picture that it is a compliment and is not embarrassed at me looking at Bermuda up close and very personal. She is unshaven and I tell her what a turn on that is after so many of today's women shave their pubes and even some men too. We discuss the shaved silicone women of today for a while before I pull her on top of me and briefly enter her womanhood before deflating for the first time in my life without full erection and climax.

My brief excitement at Liz letting me enter her without questions or concerns about a condom is thus short-lived. I am embarrassed but Liz is great in telling me not to be and we have all the time in the world to complete the act and we are both like virgins needing to learn all about sex since we both have been without sexual partners for years. She tells me again how Jerque lost interest soon after their marriage and wanted sex only about once a month while she always felt sexual and unsuccessfully tried to encourage him to have sex every night and morning.

"You like it in the morning too?" I ask and she says yes. I am turned on again because I thought most women do not like morning sex while most men wake up with hard-ons that find no relief. "Nonsense," Liz says. I rub my deflated penis on her button (clitoris) and Bermuda with one hand and she moans some more. Especially when I rub her erect nipple with my other hand and blow softly in and lick her inner ears. I love how responsive she is to all these touches. I touch and knead her rear with both hands as she lies on top of me in all her glory and laugh at her high school type rule when earlier she had let me know that I could touch her backside on the outside of her jeans but not inside. She says she needed to let me know when to stop but I said at the time I was not headed for the ultimate target but she says that obviously is a slippery slope and she was not ready for that yet. This touching and talking (T&T) is terrific I say and she says tremendous is a better word and I agree. The TNT or whatever we call it continues throughout the night and into the a.m. until almost ten o'clock the next morning. We can't get enough of each other's bodies and Liz reassures me that my paunch is minor and muscled anyway so I should forget about it as she thinks I have an Adonis body and loves every bit of it. Who am I to argue?

Now, don't touch that dial. We'll be right back with "Reverse Love Story" after this important commercial message

Memory

This account of our "first time" and the day before is almost contemporaneous with the actual events. At the time I had been concerned that I could not remember details of my early relationship with Liz, even when the details had been experienced just a few days earlier. Therefore I forced myself to journal every day for several months by describing in detail my experiences with Liz. The account of our first time therefore was written within a day of actual happening; close enough to be considered as contemporaneous. I was writing for myself with no intent to share with anyone, but just to capture and preserve the memories for myself. I was tempted to clean-up my contemporaneous account for this *Metaphors* book, but then realized something valuable would be lost in the process.

Sometimes it is better to see the forest than the trees, which perspective is provided by time and distance further from the event. It is possible, although I think highly unlikely, that future historians will validate George W. Bush's contention that his Iraq war was justified. The problem is that the further from the event, the more one forgets the look and feel of the trees and such forgetting or "winnowing" naturally takes place for all of us, young and old alike.

The details are what make a story important and valuable. In fact, it may be interesting and useful to see some of the chaff as well as the wheat (unless chaff by definition is useless). Could we be in a conspiracy with our mind to winnow out detail that might be important? Or does the winnowing enable us to see the essential? These issues probably have been written about more intelligently in the related professional literature about short-term and long-term memory, but I'm only interested in exploring my own thoughts here. If this is getting too theoretical to be of interest, just hit delete or otherwise skip past these reflections.

So is detail useful or harmful, or both depending upon the situation? In Hum 6 (see Harvard experience, Chapter 15), Professor Reuben Brower taught us to forget biographies and contemporary history (what he considered the chaff — forest), and focus just on the trees. In fact, his approach was to focus on each branch and each leaf of the tree in order to gain valuable insight into the meaning of a poem or novel. Some of Brower's colleagues considered this kind of focused analysis to be analytical overkill, destroying the very beauty and heart of the poem itself. That debate still rages. I come down mostly on Brower's side of the debate, and think it valuable to see and then analyze each tree and even each leaf if possible. I strongly believe the informed judgment and critical thinking inherent in careful analysis is crucial to the survival of our democracy, as discussed below.

Initially I had dismissed Twitter as endless mindless nonsense compounding the data avalanche. Who cares what you had for breakfast? I reconsidered when 140 characters out of Tunisia and Egypt first informed the world of the Arab Spring, and similarly now provide us with contemporaneous accounts of world events that affect all of us.

My personal journal unintentionally leads to a related thought about what I consider to be the twenty-first century challenge. It starts in our schools, as emphasized by Merle McClung in *Repurposing Education* (Kappan, May 2013):

> *In a dumbed-down age when political and economic spin*

is shameless because it is effective, the Founders' vision of the informed and active citizenry necessary to make democracy work is especially relevant. They left us with a common national purpose for education: the civic standard, incorporating our core values and a purpose larger than self. We need to find ways to adopt, implement and advance the civic standard in K-12 public schools.

But the twenty-first century challenge is even larger than indicated by McClung. All schools, public and private alike, need to dedicate their curriculum and teaching to the critical thinking necessary to make our democracy work. If your school already has a critical thinking component, review to see if it is sufficient for twenty-first century needs. Furthermore, all Americans, young and old and everyone in between, need to develop and sharpen their critical thinking skills so that our democracy can function and even thrive. The problem is aggravated by the avalanche of spin and other distracting data, from social media to various private and governmental organizations that threaten to bury us alive in misleading or irrelevant data. Switching metaphors, our citizenry needs the critical thinking skills necessary to separate the chaff from the wheat. The twenty-first century challenge is daunting, but not impossible for informed and active citizens.

The wheat/chaff metaphor is Biblical and suggests an age-old problem confronting every generation. But computers have vastly compounded the extent of the problem and as in so many other areas, computers may be needed to solve the problem. The problem is separating the chaff from the wheat or perhaps more accurately, finding a needle in a haystack. I'm looking for a metaphor more appropriate to our times than wheat/chaff or needle/haystack, but have not found one yet. The problem confronts us at all levels. Mega (big data) and micro (personal memory) but probably most important where McClung sets his focus – on the critical thinking skills necessary to see through political and economic spin in order to make our democracy work.

The twenty-first century challenge deals with a national problem threatening our democracy; at a personal level it is about searching for the essential truth about the relationship Liz and I are developing. The ease of typing, storing and retrieving endless words and pages made possible by the computer facilitated my journal expanding into over two hundred pages of single-spaced detail within four months. Once the pump was primed, it was relatively easy to write fast and to write long.

As a result I find the task of picking and choosing what to include in *Metaphors* exceedingly difficult. Less than five percent of my four-month journal makes an appearance in *Metaphors*, leaving me, and perhaps some readers, to wonder if I have made the best decisions about what to keep and what to set aside. In the end it is the author's prerogative to decide (who else?) and almost all accounts of my relationship with Liz are excerpted from my personal journal. They, along with the e-mails which have also been separated from the chaff of e-mail diarrhea we all endure, make *Metaphors* as contemporaneous an account as possible.

The relative ease in which the computer enables me to do so also leads to the problem of this book morphing from one into three volumes. The task of writing used to be, perhaps still is for the best writing, starting with a blank page. As Gene Fowler famously put it, "Writing is easy. Just stare at a blank page until you sweat blood." Today the task is just the opposite, separating overwhelming chaff from essential wheat.

One final thought before returning to the story. I think the mind must winnow away extraneous data so it does not overwhelm us. Think of a funnel where all the memories (data) are collected at the top and as time passes the mind relentlessly winnows away. In the first years the winnowing provides interesting perspective as we are better able to see the forest, but soon it creates comforting generalizations that are counterproductive. As time passes further even the generalizations become confused as we suffer from Alzheimer's, dementia and other memory and mind-destroying diseases. The wheat at the bottom of the funnel turns to mush. And then the final stage, death, when all memory is lost — forever.

I develop these reflections from writing *Metaphors*. For example, I initially think and write that Pam, my live-in girlfriend for twelve years, and I separated amicably and lived happily for a while until she met the cowboy of her dreams. As I find old notes describing the experience I remember the deep pain and anguish at the time and so will include some of it in a chapter about Pam (Chapter 13) to provide a more detailed, accurate and interesting account. So too with the description I was writing about my Harvard roommate, Don Ransom. My generalized account from my fading memory was starting to bore even me and then I found a copy of a fifteen-year-old letter I had written to Don and decided to include it (Chapter 15). The detail about the tie and surprisingly personal confession, given my previously ultra-private persona, are much closer to the reality of my experience than the dull draft I had started to write.

My recollections of Don today, fifty-three years after we met, are less detailed than in a letter I sent him seventeen years ago. My recollections today of the separation from Pam, seventeen years after the fact, are totally different from those detailed at the time. Is there a golden mean between too much and too little data somewhere in the years between an event and total loss of memory at death? Perhaps all that one needs to know is that any account of any event is not absolute, but changes continuously in the time spectrum between contemporaneous birth to ultimate death. We need to find middle ground somewhere between being lost among the leaves of trees to the perspective provided over time of seeing the forest. We can't see the trees for the forest; we can't see the forest for the trees. Perhaps somewhere in between we can learn to maximize the benefits of both.

Now back to "Reverse Love Story"

At one point Liz and I relive our first date the Sunday morning at her house and I say I loved it when she spontaneously put her arms around me and I knew then what a warm and sensual and giving woman she was and how I appreciated the fact that she did not play games with our budding relationship. So this hugging and touching and kissing was just natural and not a big thing and our whole relationship seemed natural and right this way. We laugh at Liz's spontaneous, "You can't get an erection?" after I explained to Liz that my Afib robs me of about twenty percent of my energy and blood flow. I say I'm totally charmed by her directness like when she said, "I would like to see you naked," and instead of saying the obvious that the thought is mutual, I reacted by stupidly saying she would be disappointed because of my paunch.

Liz tells me about the narcissistic Jerque Johnson and how he would always walk four steps in front of her, leaving her to humbly follow behind even when she was pregnant and how he never responded to her cry to wait for her. I tell Liz this four steps in front rather than as a team together seems to me to be a metaphor for their whole marriage based on what she has told me before and she agrees.

I look at Liz's beautiful body again and think about her sensual nature and quick and funny mind and tell her again I can't believe that Jerque would let her get away and I mean it sincerely. This beautiful sensual woman deprived of love for almost all of their eighteen years of marriage while she stayed on frustrated because she needed to raise and protect her children.

We fall asleep again and again I wake Liz up with a hard-on and this time I mount her as she opens her legs wide for me to enter her in traditional missionary position. Again we move and groan for several minutes before I deflate again without coming. We are both pleased at the progress I have been making and I compliment Liz for her starring role in this version of the Lazarus story. I say that I am not even apologetic about no foreplay before entering her these two times and say she was obviously wet and ready to receive me both times without foreplay. This has been another wonderful evening.

The next morning I walk Liz to her car and it is iced and snow all over so we scrape ice off the windows. Mike MacKensie, my next door neighbor, is shoveling snow off his driveway and we chat briefly before Liz comes over to say, "Hi, my name is Liz," before I have a chance to introduce her. Not such a bad thing to let the neighborhood know that this old man living alone in the big house in the circle had an attractive woman spend the night with him. Liz French kisses me by the car door and drives off with a wave. I go back into the house and fall asleep on my bed for hours as if I had not slept at all last night.

Liz calls back Saturday afternoon to say she could come back tonight but that it will probably be late because she has projects to finish. She arrives about 10 p.m. and she eats a fruit salad while

I eat her split pea curry dish and fruit salad in the candle-lit dining room. We retire to the sofa to watch David Mamet in the director's trailer to *The Winslow Boy,* but we get to kissing and groping and soon jettison the CD in favor of the bedroom upstairs where we continue where we left off.

We touch and talk into the night but unlike last night we fall asleep soon in a spooned position. I awake with a hard-on and wake Liz who eagerly falls on top of me and Laz stays inflated long enough for Liz to comment that she has a better feel now for how Laz will be when erect inside her and her moaning and groaning underscores the thought. I am surprised and pleased because it has been such a long time since I have been inside a woman and it feels especially good with Liz. I joke with Liz that she is to me what Jesus was to Lazarus; Liz raising Steve from the dead. I had been prepared to live without sex, but now sex is returning when least expected. Sex is not exactly like getting on a bicycle again since I have not completed the act, but progress is clearly being made. I joke with Liz that perhaps I will not need Viagra after all.

We continue to talk and touch and Liz is still wet and moaning as I caress her button with my finger first and then my deflated Laz head and her Bermuda with other fingers. She moans in pleasure as I do so and says she loves this too. This was the night that Laz came to life. Back upstairs in bed we are back to heated touching which proceeds to oral sex. Here's how it happened.

Steve, "Laz, meet Liz."

Liz, "Hi Laz, I'm Liz."

Steve, "I hope that Laz and Liz will have a long term relationship (LTR)."

Liz, "Is it OK if Liz gives Laz a kiss to mark the beginning of an LTR?"

Steve, "Looks like Laz is up for it."

Liz, kissing Laz softly, "I'm sure Liz will love Laz."

Steve, "Oh, my God! Oh, Oh."

Liz, "Thought you didn't believe in God."

Steve, "Think I'm becoming a believer. Thank you God!"

Liz, "Hey, big guy. It's not God you should thank. It's Liz."

Liz whispers into my ear that sometime she would like to take Laz in her mouth. I immediately ask, "When?"

"When would you like?" she replies.

"How about now?" I say.

So she starts to lick my chest for a while and then says, "Now don't you get lonely while I leave you for a while." This delicate way of putting it is a big turn on and I quiver in anticipation as her head and tongue move slowly down my chest and stomach to my manhood. I have never had such good head and I moan while she licks and eats me and it is all the better because she clearly enjoys it and prolongs it while I enjoy but do not climax for some reason even though at times I feel close to doing so.

I tell Liz how wonderful that was and ask if I can return the favor on Bermuda. She says, "Yes, but not now because I'm just fine." Later after I wake her after she falls asleep I go down on her and it is wonderful because as I lick and suck her button (the little guy in the boat) and then Bermuda and then back to her button again, she moans responsively. I prolong this oral sex as she did with me earlier and all seems right with the world. Later in the early morning hours as we continue to put our hands all over each other, Liz asks if I would like her to do anything in particular and I say, "You remember that nice thing you did earlier, that would be nice again." Again, she goes down on me and I am in heaven again. She says she does not mind my waking her; in fact I am free to wake her anytime for more of the same. She says she will give me oral sex anytime I want it and I ask, "Anytime?" and she qualifies it by saying, "Anytime in private." I say, "That works for me." I can live with that qualification. We agree that it is a shame to waste any time sleeping when we are in bed together, we can sleep anytime. But we do sleep for a little while as I lay on my right side spooning her very close into me with my arms around her and one hand holding an ample breast. Can this get any better? Liz is the complete package and I tell her so with great appreciation and admiration.

My expanded wish list included a woman who does not play the usual "chase me until I catch you" games. Fortunately Liz fills that wish as she seems so open and honest and direct in initiating many sexual pleasures. When I wake in the middle of the night she turns into me with open arms eager for Laz. She says she loves sex with me at any time and any place and I know she means it even though I joke, "How about at noon at the club swimming pool?" This love of sex extends to the tricks she does with her tongue on Laz and the magical lengths she stays with it and almost all of our sexual play includes lengthy sessions of such. I thank God (I am a believer!) that I come in her mouth in rare orgasm and she swallows with the explanation, "Why wouldn't I?" I especially like this because I have heard of wives who promise their husbands a blowjob on their birthday and then do so in disgust to get it over with quickly. Since it is obviously not mutual pleasure, such birthday blowjobs must lose their point and pleasure.

A few nights later, Liz makes me a chicken curry dinner at her house. The meal as usual was delicious and I suggest we watch Jon Stewart's *Daily Show* but we agree that would take our focus off each other. Soon we are groping again and Liz asks if I want to go upstairs to bed. I of course immediately agree saying that I have been fantasizing about trying out her antique sleigh bed. So we continue with the touching and hugging in her bed but she says she needs sleep and has much work to do so I must leave by midnight. I agree and expect to do so and say that Laz has had such a workout the past few days that nothing much can happen anyway. This turns out to be untrue and we manage to connect several times before I mysteriously deflate again before orgasm. We discuss whether this is due to my virgin status or perhaps the reduced blood flow to extremities caused by my Afib. Liz is not concerned as she says she enjoys all the foreplay, so all is more than well.

About midnight I prepare to leave as agreed but on the way out I cannot find my car keys. We retrace all my steps since arrival including outside in the dark night but cannot find the keys. I apologize profusely and assure her this is not a ploy to stay longer and she knows that is the case. Liz sensibly suggests I stay with her until morning when it is light enough to see if I have dropped the keys outside in or near my car. I find it hard to sleep knowing that I might have to get my 1996 Camry towed and rekeyed. About 5 a.m. I wake and go through my sneakers again where I find the keys underneath the thin pad inside one of my sneakers. We are both relieved to find the keys but wonder how I could have walked around the house without feeling the keys pressing against my foot. Liz suggests this could be lack of blood supply and feeling to extremities caused by Afib and this seems plausible. I ask Liz if she wants me to go but she says she thinks I might as well stay until morning now. And a good thing too, because our sensual hugging and groping gets better and better and we find a delicious new sexual position a step beyond spooning which Liz calls "spoonary" as the counterpart to missionary sex and I stay hard for a long time without orgasm. Liz says she also enjoys missionary sex because she likes to look at and feel my body pressing against hers when I lay on her with my full weight. I have been reluctant to do so for fear of squashing her but she encourages me to try and says not doing so is a wall I am unilaterally creating that needs to be replaced with a window and she will tell me if and when I get too heavy on top of her.

Liz suggests that perhaps Laz could use some special attention with her tongue tricks before I leave and I tell her I have been fantasizing about just that. Then shortly before I leave at 8 a.m. Liz pays Laz a visit and has several new tongue and mouth tricks that have me swooning with pleasure. I tell her she has jumped several grades since the last visit with Laz. Again, what makes all this foreplay and afterplay is the mutuality of it. Liz really enjoys all of it including lengthy visits with Laz. Once again I think about the cliché of wives reluctantly giving their husbands a birthday blowjob but not really liking the experience themselves. Not Liz! I laugh with the sheer joy of it all and at one point after Liz gets up in the night naked as the overhead light casts dark shadows over her body and she looks so magnificent that I say that she is my complete package (meaning body and mind and everything else). She knows what I mean and I think she is very pleased too. I drive home about 8 a.m. relieved to have found my keys and even more pleased that the lost keys led to the best sexual experience we have shared yet.

dream cycles

Before you sleep tonight my little one
I'll tell you of the Sickles in the sun.
Head of the family was Pop Sickle,
Cold and hard, he once sold for a nickel,
But with inflationary increments
His price went all the way to forty cents.
He called his gentle wife Ma Dream Sickle,
Married Pop when he tickled her stick,
And gave her a kiss instead of a lick.
Like a ripe peach was her exterior
With cool ice cream for an interior.
A small son called Fudge Sickle they begat.
He was sweet throughout like dark chocolate.
Since Fudge was sometimes bad and somewhat fat
Kids called him Pudge Sickle because of that.
They nicked his name in ways Fudge tried forget
Like Little Lickle Stickle and Not Et Yet.
Fudge cried "I'll neither be et nor upset
Since your nicknames just prove poor etiquette."
Yet for all their teasing and chitter-chat,
Kids liked Fudge a lot since he was chocolate.

Chapter 5
POOR BOY

"Education is not the filling of a bucket,
But the starting of a fire."
—William Butler Yeats

Michigan Background

I grew up the second of five children in Milan, a small Michigan town (population about 5,800). We lived in a small three-bedroom "Sears catalogue" wood-frame house that was slowly deteriorating from deferred maintenance. My earliest memories are of loud fights between my working mother and my deadbeat father who drank away the little money he earned doing odd jobs as an unskilled laborer rather than helping to support the family. As long as I can remember, the toilet and the furnace in the house were broken, unusable and never repaired since there was hardly enough money for food, much less for a toilet or furnace repair. We heated the house during the long freezing Michigan winters with a kerosene heater, which could not even heat the entire kitchen in which it stood.

Another early memory as a kid is walking to the corner filling station almost every winter day with a quarter in hand to refill a gallon tin with kerosene for the heater, and then using the station's toilet, as did my two brothers and two sisters. We were embarrassed as well as grateful when a church group would bring us a charitable basket of food for Christmas, confirming our plight as one of the town's poorest families. One winter my mother's father butchered one of his farm hogs, cut it through the middle from snout to tail and delivered half of the hog with half head still attached, to our house for food. We did not have a freezer, so I remember for weeks afterward stepping around the half hog lying lifeless on a blanket on the floor of our living room. It seemed bizarre even at the time, but the unheated room served well as a natural freezer and it was one time when we ate both high and low off the hog. The dirt floor basement, which housed the broken furnace, also served as a natural freezer and my mother would can and jar tomatoes and other vegetables from our backyard garden to store in shelves against one wall. I did not care much for the canned string beans, but the shelves of tomatoes would never last through the winter as I would often grab a spoon and devour a whole jar at one sitting.

My mother encouraged us to work by saying that anything we earned we could keep for ourselves. One summer when I was about eight years old I earned nickels and dimes pulling a wagon filled with pumpkins I had grown to be sold to neighbors, and spent most of the proceeds on candy bars. My first real job at age eleven was working for a milkman who delivered milk to nearby towns in his refrigerated van. He would honk his horn outside our house about five a.m. on cold dark mornings and I would crawl half-asleep into the back of the van and hand him milk bottles at his various stops. It sounds unreal now, but I was grateful for the fifty cents per day he paid as wages.

This milk truck experience put me in line for a promotion the next year working for the milkman who delivered in town and doubled my wages from fifty cents to one dollar a day. He would drive the milk truck and I would deliver the milk to the front steps of houses, and thus get to meet customers and even make change. A fringe benefit was the fudge sickles, dream sickles, pop sickles

Author's $1 a day job

and ice cream bars he would "steal" from the company ice cream truck and then give to me with great ceremony as he pulled one treat after another from his various pockets. He also delighted in shocking me with his oft-repeated quips such as, "That guy thinks his shit doesn't stink, but his farts give him away." Then he would laugh and laugh as though it was a first time telling and the funniest joke in the world.

The worst job I ever had was one summer working for my uncle on his poorly run farm. The work was exhausting and I remember standing at the front of a hay wagon pulled by a hay bailer shooting bales out of its rear end chute that I would spike with a steel hook and stack in the back of the wagon. The work was almost intolerable in the summer heat as the baler would throw dust as well as bales back toward my sweaty body, and I soon resolved to get enough education never to have to do that kind of miserable farm work again. At the end of the summer my uncle procrastinated when I asked him for the fifty dollars he had promised in wages. He told me that he would have to pay me later, but then made excuses and then several weeks later told me that I had been paid enough since he had provided me with room and board during my "vacation." The board consisted of scrambled eggs for breakfast, egg sandwich for lunch and an egg dish for dinner every day; so many eggs that I could have taken on Paul Newman in *Cool Hand Luke*. My uncle never paid me a dime, but it was a valuable learning experience.

My desire to get a good education was also reinforced by my mother who emphasized that education offered us the way to a better life. At the time she had a genuine respect for public school teachers and taught me to respect them as professionals who could help me better myself. (Poem 26, pg 165). It was a Horatio Alger message and it stuck. From grade school through high school I respected most of my teachers, and did my homework diligently while many of my more fortunate classmates could not be bothered. They had time and money for parties and play and satisfactory options for their futures. I did not and was probably too serious about life. So I was socially apart but my classmates did not dare to bully me because I was always a big, strong kid and later a respected athlete who lettered in five sports.

I was a quiet introspective kid, and did not talk much beyond what was minimally necessary. I observed that those who talked the most usually had the least to say, and the talkers usually were not the doers. I memorized the old saw that, "It is better to remain silent and thought a fool than to speak and remove all doubt." People who got respect were the doers, not the talkers, whether it was on the athletic field, battlefield, job or community service. Shakespeare's Coriolanus is structured around the same theme, and years later my Harvard thesis would focus on Coriolanus and his combative hot-headed counterparts found throughout Shakespeare's works. Talk is cheap and actions speak louder than words. Children should be seen and not heard. Refrains heard often in rural Michigan where the worst kind of talk was self-centered or bragging talk. Self-promotion was considered a character flaw, and no one liked a self-promoter. Far better to do well and leave appraisal to others. Even in later years I refused to self-promote, even though in today's world self-promotion is almost a prerequisite for success. Today's mantra it seems is inflate your resume, exaggerate achievements and invent degrees if necessary in order to promote yourself into a better job and greater compensation. I write this realizing that much of this book could be considered self-promoting, so I am adapting; even if it is too late for my career.

But there was another reason why I did not talk much. I had an embarrassing lisp in my speech, which would distract from what I was saying or trying to say. My chemistry teacher inadvertently came to my rescue one day when asking the class to recite from the periodic table. Most of the class, including myself, stumbled on the hard to pronounce — aluminum. Mr. Ted Noyes insisted that we all could pronounce the word correctly if we broke it down into syllables, "a - lu - min - um." He had us practice saying the syllables separately, and then putting them together, and within minutes most of us could pronounce the word correctly. It was a lesson about words and speaking that I took to heart and soon my lisp disappeared as I concentrated on pronouncing words and sentences with emphasis on each syllable. I continued to be a person of few words and my Michigan monotone would persist, but I was less afraid to speak now that I had acquired some confidence in speaking correctly.

I did not have to self-promote. Basketball was a sport where others would praise my deeds in the sports pages and community. I loved the game, and my play included countless hours of practice year-round on hoops attached to neighborhood garages. Basketball enabled an escape from the grim world of poverty and I was in a dream world of my own shooting baskets. My determined practice paid off as I became quite skilled at the game and this undoubtedly encouraged my high school basketball coach to give me the best job I had worked to that point. He paid me one dollar for the forty minutes or so it took to mop the boy's locker room in the school's basement. The work had to be done in the early morning before school started, but I did not mind because rather than a whole day, I now could earn a dollar for only about half an hour's work. Also, the public school was well heated during the winter days, a welcome fringe benefit. So I would go to school early to mop the locker room floor and then finish my homework at a desk in the vacant study hall on the second floor. Since it was still dark on those cold winter mornings, I would turn on one set of the study hall's fluorescent lights. This routine worked well until one morning a teacher walked into the room and turned the lights out. I looked up in surprise. She said, "What are you doing here?"

"I'm doing my homework," I replied.

"You are also wasting taxpayer money by using these lights."

I did not know what to say, so I said nothing, but even then I knew that at most I was wasting only a few pennies of the taxpayers' money. She told me to "Leave, and never let me catch you wasting electricity again." So she was one teacher I never liked or respected after that, but in later years I qualified my opinion because she also taught me how to type in her typing class. Unlike algebra and calculus, my typing skills have proved valuable throughout a lifetime of work.

When I was thirteen, I threw my father out of our house. I yelled after him to never come back. He never did and I never laid eyes on him again, even though he found nearby refuge in a flophouse downtown. The night I threw him out he had come home drunk, broke and abusive once again, but this time the abuse turned physical as he pushed and hit my mother several times. It was an ugly scene and I'd had enough. It was easy for me to physically throw him out as he was a skinny little man with no grit, and I was young, tall and strong by then. But the psychology of it was not so easy because I realized it was not my place to make this decision.

I felt better days later when my mother confided in me that she'd had enough of him as well and had decided to divorce him anyway. Years later my siblings confirmed that the family was much better off after he and all the drunken fights were gone. I thought I was unique in throwing a deadbeat dad out of a house, but in later years I read a biography of Bill Clinton and discovered that he also had done so. Some psychiatrists would see an Oedipal pattern here, but I don't think that fits the reality. I just wanted to protect my mother.

I knew at the time that the world is not black and white, but usually gray and there are at least two sides to every story, but I could not help but see my mother as the personification of good and my father as bad. Today he probably would be seen as an alcoholic who needed treatment and compassion rather than scorn and isolation. My two brothers visited him often in his waning years because they felt sorry for him, but said they had no respect for him either, and recounted subsequent examples of his drinking, lying, stealing and cheating.

In a small town everyone knows everyone and most of their business. My father was a sad joke and the community felt sorry for us and disdain for him. I do not remember any substantive conversation with him. I frequently reflected on the fact that I never learned anything from him and was surprised when Liz said the same thing about her Harvard-educated father. Ironically, Liz has a much more difficult time with her father because the problems never got resolved and so persist to this day. I had it easier as I never saw and rarely thought about my so-called father after throwing him out of the house.

I say I never learned anything from my father, but I did learn one important thing; not to be like him. I swore I would never be like him, and my primary goal in life became to earn the respect of others through hard work. More than love, much more than love, I wanted people to respect me.

I have always hoped that he in fact was not my biological father, and that my true father was the mailman or someone else, anyone but him. I could never ask my mother about this because the implication of her possible infidelity would have been offensive, given her religious beliefs. I didn't care about that implication personally as I had jettisoned her indefensible religious beliefs by that time.

I do not mean to imply that my mother or I could do no wrong or that we were bonded in some kind of Oedipal dilemma. We argued about two things, my girlfriend and her religion. We would have fights about my demand for independence and the right to stay at my girlfriend's house until two in the morning. And we would argue about religion. One day my mother invited our minister, the Reverend Howard Sherman, to our house to talk some religious sense into me. I was not inclined to like him as his stiff and dreary and endless sermons on Sunday mornings was one of the reasons I had decided it made more sense to sleep in rather than go to church.

Now standing in the kitchen of our modest house, the Reverend Howard Sherman seemed out of time and place. The sixty-some year old man, somberly dressed in a black suit and white dress shirt buttoned tight almost to his stone-set jaw, unsmiling face capped with a full head of carefully combed white hair, projected an authoritarian figure not to trifle with. His personality and religion were as black and white as his colorless attire. In sum, not someone you would want to have a beer with.

Each time I challenged him about the biblical miracles I doubted, he would quote what he considered relevant verses (Doubting Thomas, for example, was resurrected) from the open Bible he held chest high in front of him as if it were a cross or talisman to ward off Lucifer at an exorcism — I of course being the Lucifer in this scenario. I politely asked the Reverend to put away his Bible, as I needed rational persuasion rather than quotations from a Bible I was inclined not to believe. Unused to being challenged, red-faced in frustration and clearly confounded, the Reverend's reliance on scripture was the only way he knew how to address religious questions.

I did not say that I thought religion was Santa Claus for adults, but that was the gist of it as later in life I embraced the more sophisticated and believable arguments advanced by Christopher Hitchens in *God is not Great* and Richard Dawkins in *The God Delusion*. The titles alone would have given my mother a heart attack. She was not pleased with my insubordination and apologized to the Reverend as he made his escape.

My mother literally cried, "Some people think you're smart, but you're not. You are ignorant about the most important thing in life since you have not taken Jesus Christ as your Savior." Fortunately for her, my youngest brother, Matthew (Matt) fulfilled my mother's greatest wish by becoming a missionary and to this day all of my siblings with good intent say that they pray for me every night. Garrison Keillor would recognize them as totally decent "Minnesota-nice" Christians, and they are. We get along well in a superficial way, but live in different worlds.

My mother's religious message did not stick, but part of another message did. One day I overheard her scold my oldest sister who had proclaimed her love for a boy and my mother sternly told her that love is teenage nonsense, and the only lasting love is for Jesus Christ. I already believed that love of Christ was adult nonsense, but her broken marriage testified to the transitory nature of romantic love, and I had witnessed the devastation up close and personal. I also observed that very few married couples in our small town seemed happy. So I decided early on to pursue respect rather than love and this no doubt is one of the reasons why, even though I tend to put most women on the same pedestal as my marvelous mother, I never married. It is also the reason why later in life I was and am receptive to the arguments advanced by L. Kipnis in *Against Love*.

My mother's priorities were children first, religion a close second and public education a distant third. But she was a strong supporter of public schools, and firmly believed that education was a transformative power of which her children could take advantage, and improve their socio-economic status (SES). In other words, we could lift ourselves by our own bootstraps with education. As such, she taught us to respect and value our teachers, and this became a self-fulfilling prophecy (see Chapter 14).

One high school teacher stands out above all the rest. How Claude Karsazi came to Milan, Michigan from Lebanon must be a fascinating story, but none of us knew. What we did know was that Mr. Karsazi was loved by almost everyone in town and in school, including the students. This was especially ironic because Mr. Karsazi appeared worse than a nerd; he closely resembled an adult, bald Alfred E. Neuman — from *Mad Magazine*. That in itself was a valuable lesson — do not judge people by their appearance. Do not judge a book by its cover.

Mr. Karsazi loved to teach English, especially Shakespeare. His enthusiasm for Shakespeare, and the moral and political relevance of the plays to contemporary life, was contagious. Even the turned-off kids, who long ago had taken a pass at caring for education and were just marking time until they could escape their socially enforced prison, became excited with issues Mr. Karsazi raised from the texts of *Julius Caesar* and *Romeo and Juliet*. In fact, Mr. Karsazi took great pride in reaching the turned-off crowd. He was far less interested in the motivated high achieving students like me. It did not matter, as Mr. Karsazi's enthusiasm touched us all, the turned-on as well as the turned-off. This is education at its finest. This is what education is meant to be. Far from the mind and soul-killing experience of rote and other uninspired learning too often the rule, Mr. Karsazi's class exemplified what William Butler Yeats had in mind when he wrote "Education is not the filling of a bucket, but the starting of a fire." Mr. Karsazi lit fires.

A bachelor with plenty of free time in a socially conventional small town, Mr. Karsazi often would invite students to his home in the afternoons after class to discuss issues that concerned them. I was too busy lettering in five sports to be able to take advantage of Mr. Karsazi's hospitality, but one rainy day I joined some friends at his home. I still remember him saying, you have to hear this, and then I see his fingers gently lowering the phonograph needle down onto the edge of a 33 1/3 LP album. Suddenly the small living room was filled with the powerful voice of Mahalia Jackson. I had always loved church music; the only thing I liked about church. But this was another league altogether. I had never heard anything like it. As usual, I did not say anything, but my eyes filled with tears, which is saying a lot for someone raised on the icy stoicism so pervasive in the small corner of my southeastern Michigan world. I don't think anything inside our public school opened my world as much as that one recording in Mr. Karsazi's modest living room.

Graduating from Mr. Karsazi's sophomore English class to Mr. Anderson's English class for juniors was a big step back down into reality, but Mr. Anderson did the best he could. One day his lesson emphasized the necessity for perspective on the world, including a que-sera-sera philosophy to help endure the world's hardships. What will be will be? Mr. Anderson should not be teaching his students that. It was one of the few times I raised my hand to speak.

Mr. Anderson, "Yes, Steve, you have a question?"

Steve, "Yes sir, if we all followed the que-sera-sera message, nothing would ever get done in the world. All progress would stop. It's a false message I hear in church; don't worry, God will provide. I think we need to provide for ourselves, and get out and change the world."

Mr. Anderson, "You make a good point, but perhaps you over-state the case? The class writing assignment due on Monday will be on whether Steve is right about que-sera-sera. No complaining; at least ten pages on the topic."

The class groaned, and gave me a look that said — this is the first time all year you open your big mouth, and now we all pay for it. My paper that Monday concluded with something like, "We can use these lessons as stepping stones to a better future." Mr. Anderson's handwritten comments were, "I'm giving you an "A" again, but this paper is the best thing you have written yet for my class. Nice metaphor helps you make your point."

I thought with surprise, he's right, that is quite good, and I wrote it. I wrote it in study hall on Friday morning after mopping the locker room floor. Perhaps I can be a writer some day.

Just Rewards

Some think today's sport salaries a sorry shame
A million or more a year just to play a game
To kick a ball or push a puck into a net
Throw a fit or stuff a round ball through a basket
Pitch a curve, steal a base, hit homeruns with a bat
When doctors, lawyers and captains of industry
Must work hard to squeeze by on less than half of that.
Others disagree with such sense of economy:
Consider the fortunes made by the rock star's scream,
To host talk shows or make blood and gore for the screen,
Not to mention the pusher's score or insider's trade.
All things considered, athletes may be underpaid.
My only complaint, and it really makes me sore:
For some money is only a way to keep score,
But if true merit is rewarded as before,
Then folk like you and me should make as much — or more.

Chapter 6
PAUL'S VISIT

When I had been with Liz long enough (about three weeks) to sense that we might have a long-term relationship (LTR), I decided it was time to let my best friend, Paul, know about Liz. Paul K. Bryant, two years ahead of me at Harvard College and later Harvard Law School (HLS), is now a prominent tax attorney at a big prestigious law firm in downtown Los Angeles, and as a result, a member of the one-percent class. Paul is also my alter-persona since he convinced his firm to make me an offer without an interview years ago, and so I see in his career and success what my life probably would have been like if I had accepted the offer. I know he will be delighted to hear that I have found Liz after ten years as a bachelor who was not even looking very hard for a match. And he is as happy to hear, as I was to relay, the news when I call him. He wants to know all about Liz.

I tell him, "Liz is a three-letter Harvard jock who is fourteen years younger than me, and I told her that she would probably jettison me at some point because of our age difference. What convinced me that Liz was worth changing my solitary life for," I tell Paul, was her smart-ass response; "Get real, Steve. If I wanted to jettison you, there are a hundred other reasons."

We hang up, and Paul calls back within twenty minutes to inform me that he has rescheduled his flight from a speaking engagement in Minneapolis, and will be paying me a visit in three days. "I want to meet this woman," he says, "to make sure she is good enough for you."

Paul's visit presents a logistical dilemma when Liz asks me when I am going to pick him up at the airport. I tell her that I don't plan to pick Paul up since Denver International Airport (DIA) is forty miles and an hour drive from my house. Liz is appalled that I would not extend this customary courtesy to my friend.

I explain that I find it a pain to pick someone up at DIA since I am that rare bird without a cell phone, and thus timing the pick-up is difficult and would lead to additional inconvenience. I admit that this is one of the few times when I could use a cell phone (emergencies are another). Looking disgusted, Liz retorts, "No, you're more like a dinosaur." I may be eccentric, but I don't consider myself a dinosaur or a Luddite either, for that matter — just a firm believer that a cell phone doesn't make sense for me. Unlike Liz, I don't have children or friends with whom I need to be in contact 24/7, and my landline with voice mail serves me just fine.

I consider cell phones an unnecessary leash impinging upon my freedom. Liz knows that I had negotiated a cut in pay and position (from full-time assistant professor on a tenure track to part time assistant professor on a dead-end track) with the Dean in trade for freedom from committees, staff meetings and other customary onerous obligations. I explained to the Dean that time was more important to me than money or position. When he agreed, but later handed me a cell phone paid for by the university, I felt betrayed. The cell phone was a 24/7 leash violating our agreement that I would give the university less rather than more of my time. When the cell phone was never used, he asked me to return it.

"Besides," I said, "since Paul is a friend, he will understand." And he did, declining my offer to pay for a taxi; he said it would be easier for him to rent a car as his law firm had a sweetheart deal with Hertz.

Three days later Paul is ringing my doorbell. Liz opens the door, and Paul says: "Hi Liz, I'm 102." Liz and I laugh, knowing that reason Number 101 is our age difference. Thereafter Paul is known as 102, or just 02 as Liz suggests, and thus the nickname extends the joke to all future contacts. We chat for awhile in the kitchen where Liz is preparing a pork chop dinner for us, and then Liz suggests we get out of her way: "Why don't you two go out on the porch and catch up on all your guy stuff."

So we step out onto the porch and do exactly that. Paul and I always have stimulating and enjoyable conversations. We start by comparing notes on the Denver Nuggets and Los Angeles Clippers. Paul used to have season tickets to the Lakers, but traded them for Clipper tickets after Kobe Bryant, Paul's namesake, had his infamous and expensive run-in with the law at a resort hotel in Edwards, Colorado. Now he detests the Lakers with passion, referring to Kobe as "the rapist" and the Lakers as "the rapist Lakers." After some additional small talk about mutual friends, Paul surprises me.

Paul, "You know, Steve, I envy you."

Steve, "You have to be kidding."

Paul, "No, I mean it; in part because you have no debt, and you take advantage of your absurd amount of free time. I have pain-in-the-ass alimony payments and a two million dollar mortgage."

Steve, "You also have an absurd net worth, and you could pay off that mortgage tomorrow by selling a small fraction of your portfolio. You don't do so because our absurd tax laws allow you, like the average Jack and Jane who need it more, to deduct most of your mortgage payments. The U.S. government in absurd effect is helping you pay the absurd mortgage on your absurd McMansion."

Paul, "Don't forget the State of California provides similar absurd help. I agree with you that tax law is inequitable, and the law in its' majestic equality forbids the rich just like the poor from stealing bread. But I would be foolish not to take advantage."

Steve, "I know. I'm venting against the system, not you personally."

Paul, "If you organize a group to change the law, hire a lobbyist or whatever, I'll send you a substantial check. We're not all bad guys, you know."

Steve, "I know."

I also know, because Paul confided in me, that a few years ago when a rival law firm was trying to persuade him to jump ship and join their team, in order to get them off his back he boldly stated that it would take a million dollar annual salary to do so. The next morning he received another call from them: "What else do you need?" A few days later Paul was shown a corner office in his new LA law firm.

Steve, "I know that you are as concerned as I that extreme income inequality is tearing apart the social fabric that ties us together as a nation."

Paul (starting to boil over with anger), "You think my mortgage deductions are shitty. What really pisses me off is the tax law that permits the fucking greedheads at hedge funds and investment banks to treat their earned income as capital gain, and thus their tax rate is substantially lower than Warren Buffet's secretary."

Steve, "Did you see the Polk article in the *New York Times* about the Wall Street trader who admitted he was deeply disappointed that his last annual bonus came to only three and a half million dollars?"

Paul, "Yes, he characterizes them as money addicts who have no compassion for the poor, and the greedy fuckers are likely to continue to buy influence in Congress and state legislatures to protect what they have and get even more."

Steve, "I know you recommended Michael Lewis' *The Big Short*, and it's on my reading list, along with the other two you recommended: *Too Big to Fail* by Andrew Sorkin, and Daniel Brown's *Boys in a Boat*."

Paul and I share a love of reading, and we do a lot of it. This is not surprising in my case because I have so much free time, relatively speaking, to read. Paul must fit his reading into a busy professional schedule. Over the years I have found that Paul's book recommendations almost never disappoint.

Recently we agreed to trade recommendations of three books each, since shared books usually lead to great conversations. My recommendations were *A Sense of Ending* by Julian Barnes, *Strangers* by Anita Brookner, and Lee Child's *Killing Floor*. Paul tends to read mostly nonfiction, especially if it is counter-intuitive like Daniel Pink's *Drive* or *The Drunkard's Walk* by Leonard Mlodinow. I encourage Paul to read more fiction: thus the three books I recommended.

Paul, "So Steve, you know I recommended Michael Lewis' *Big Short*?"

Steve, "Can't wait to read it. Heard it's really good. I mean a really good book about bad practices."

Paul, "*The Big Short's* such ancient history. Flying in this afternoon I heard Lewis discussing his new book *Flash Boys* – another expose on Wall Street greed like *Liar's Poker,* only this time the greedheads' manipulation of the market is even more outrageous."

Steve, "No way."

Paul, "Way. Lewis tells the story of this amazing young Canadian trader, Ken Katsuyama, who was mystified that every time he tried to buy stocks for his clients at the prices offered on his computer screen, the offers would instantly vanish and the prices pop higher. Long story, but Katsuyama and colleagues discovered that some predatory pricks, *Flash Boys* is Lewis' metaphor for them, had rigged the system with their sophisticated instantaneous trading scheme."

Steve, "Rigged? How?"

Paul, "Get this. The fuckers purchase trading information from other greedheads at the exchanges and then use that information to buy stocks milliseconds before the trade is complete."

Steve, "Sounds like insider trading to me."

Paul, "Sure does, only it's legal."

Steve, "You've got to be shitting me."

Paul, "No, for real. Some kinds of `fronting the market,' as it is called, are illegal, but not this new kind.

Steve, "Where is Elizabeth Warren when we need her?"

Paul, "The same greedheads who profit from this scheme are the ones who lobbied her out of contention."

Steve, "So all the greedheads are in bed together. What a country!"

Paul, "Absolutely. What really gets me is that the greedheads at the exchanges are selling their customer information to further line their pockets and the trading volumes are so huge that the predatory pricks can afford to pay it and still make a nice profit."

Steve, "Not a nice profit. A nasty profit. When the public hears about this, the shit is going to hit the fan. They are going to be so pissed."

Paul, "Would you consider that a mixed metaphor?"

Steve, "Shit and piss? I guess so."

Paul, "Sure it will be a big time scandal. Talking heads, op eds, nightly news, etc. 24/7 until something new comes along. Then the current scandal takes a back seat to the latest scandal and the pattern keeps repeating itself with only band-aids, if anything, as the remedy."

Steve, "Yes we wouldn't want anyone interfering with the free market would we?"

Paul, "Exactly – that's the next step. Spin the problem, create a smoke screen, blame the victims, screw the…"

Steve, "Speaking of mixed metaphors, I would like to enter you in a contest for same. The pattern seems clear enough. The greedheads will continue to invent new predatory schemes faster than Michael Lewis can expose them."

Paul, "The bottom line is that the greedheads never have enough. Most are rich beyond our imaginations and yet they kick and claw for even more, while the poor can go to jail for stealing bread to feed their families."

Steve, "Remember the conversations we used to have about `how much is enough'?"

Paul, "Yes, we talked about income inequality increasing at a faster pace since the Reagan era. Extreme income inequality is not only a U.S. problem. Did you see that recent report which showed that the world's eighty-five richest people have wealth equal to that of the poorest half of all humans?"

Steve, "Yes. It's pervasive, on a world-wide scale. Did you ever watch the Inside Job documentary showing the world's financial crisis starting with banks in Iceland?"

Paul, "No, I haven't. This is getting fucking depressing. I was going to download *The Wolf of Wall Street* to read on the plane to-morrow morning, but now I'm more in the mood to read *The Killing Floor.* Are there any more world problems for us to solve?"

Steve, "Probably. Actually I have some thoughts about defining "enough" in terms of financial independence."

Paul, "Care to elaborate?",

Steve, "I need to think it through more carefully. Maybe I can pick your alleged brain about it sometime later?"

Liz (calling from inside), "Hey Oh-Two, did you bring an appetite? Dinner's ready."

Lots of laughs were shared over a candle-lit dinner that night, and the pork chops with basmati rice and caramelized carrots delicious, eliciting well-deserved praise.

Liz, "Well Paul, you must be exhausted after all your travel today. And I know that listening to all Steve's bullshit can be tiring. So why don't we call it an early night? I'll show you to the guest room."

Paul, "I know the way. And I also know you are getting rid of me early so you two can play around. Just keep it down a bit, if you can manage. I do need my beauty sleep."

Liz, "I don't know if Steve can keep it down, but I'll do my part."

On that note Paul retreated to the guest room, and Liz and I jumped into my king-size bed — and fell asleep, and did not wake until about five the next morning, at which time Laz was definitely up for some play. Liz was more than willing, and worked her usual magic before we fell asleep again. About seven in the morning Liz woke me, saying it was about time for me to get up to say goodbye to our guest, but we both fell asleep again and did not wake until after nine. Downstairs on the kitchen island we found a note thanking us for a good time. Paul had left an hour earlier to catch his plane, and Liz was appalled and embarrassed once again by my hosting shortcomings.

Liz, "I'm so embarrassed. You did not even say goodbye to your friend."

Steve, "Because he's my friend, he'll understand. At the very least he will give me the benefit of doubt."

Liz, "If you don't call him immediately to apologize, I will."

Steve, "OK, I guarantee you that an apology is not necessary, but you should call him if you want. Perhaps you should wait until after his plane has landed."

Paul, like me also in a similar situation, could care less about a goodbye or an apology. By making a big deal of it and showing her embarrassment, however, Liz had given Paul a nice little parting gift. Paul and I immediately knew what Liz could not see because she was on the other side of the gender gap. So I was not surprised that Paul would milk the embarrassment on every private and public occasion thereafter, "Those lovebirds could not even get out of bed long enough to say goodbye!"

Fox and Field

An open field a walk from where we live
Offers the best views the mountains can give
And a canal cutting a horseshoe bend
Lined with cottonwoods that still attend
Its easy flow and gradually grow
From seeds scattered a century ago.
Its waters continue the nourishment
Of environment to such extent
We can still hear the meadowlark sing
And watch the prairie falcon take wing
While great horned owl crouched in half-dead tree
With eyes designed especially to see
Rodent and rabbit running randomly
And the full degree of this anomaly
In place and time, a prior destiny.
One wet morning it was our privilege
To face pregnant fox all red on the ridge
Framed statuesque to show her condition
Than vanished as if an apparition.

Dark smoke today in field swirling skyward
Field fires set by order of landlord
Burn until the ground is black and barren
And then surveyed and staked to prepare an
Apt transition for new subdivision.
One corner not burned by this decision
Where on the ridge the red fox once again
Looking back to her den and what had been
And perhaps to a better time when
She could run free of all premonition.
We have never seen each other again
Yet she haunts us with her apparition.

Chapter 7
REVERSE LOVE STORY: STEVE AND LIZ

Contrasts by Liz
Contrasts in our relative situations growing up:

Bathrooms
Steve's family in Milan, Michigan
Eliza's family Boston, Massachusetts

Mothers
Fathers
Sibling relationships

Religion
1. *as part of our world view, growing up and now*
2. *end of life issues, last chapter*

Naming Laz and Bermuda, using these names as foils, as is done w/ children and talking about difficult issues. Puppets.

Marriage
Steve – never wanted
Older brother's high school shotgun, how it affected Steve's outlook for opportunities and life

Eliza – pangs from divorce
Surprised was getting married on overseas trip

Loyalty

The First Time
EW remembers it all. The Second Time "I did that already."
Steve can't recall. The blessing of the pill.

"But I want to say that I'm not looking for anyone or anything."

Our first live encounter, not a date, but highly anticipated
He likes touch. EW puts arms around him.
He tells EW about Afib. Response: "Does that mean it's difficult
for you to have an erection?"
Or are you sickly?

EW, "I'm looking forward to seeing you naked."
Two dates later she drops trous in the front hall.

High School sexual awareness, or not
All-girls high school vs. active dating
First French kiss. Cornfield & curtains in car & farmer w/ gun.

Mars/Venus: talking at crossed purposes
"Washing the dog" vs. "Watching the dog"
Interpretation of Relationship Wish List: #6 expressing mutuality
vs. interpreting it as narcissistic
Breaking It Down: first 3rd Friday at BAC, doing lay ups, breaking
down the minutiae of each action in order to understand the whole.

Resurrecting our tennis games after 35 years
1. *hitting*
2. *short hitting at net*

3. *focusing on consistency*
4. *counting: 68 = "69"*
5. *getting the groove*
6. *The Harder They Come, EW thrives on the challenge, doesn't care if gets hit.*

Mutuality vs. Obliviousness

No mutuality vs. "It's the key to everything."

Four Steps Behind

Starts two days after our wedding. Also, when pregnant. He knows I hate him walking ahead, still does it, why can't he help himself? Last time this happened when we went to his office xmas party. I'm wondering, once again, and decide the best way to cope and keep some self-respect is to slow down, be 20 steps behind, and pretend that I'm not associated with him at all. Have my own separate entrance.

US Law re: obliviousness

The exception of US Law for retarded and insane; you're excused if you can't tell right from wrong. Does that apply to narcissists?

As I am writing this, my breasts are swooping onto the page, I feel Laz pressing against me from behind.

Cleaning exercise. Steve gives quite a bit of grief. "I washed the kitchen floor last year! Is it dirty?" "OK, so it'll get washed again on June 20th next year." EW wants to clean the countertops, asks Steve to move the cookbooks. Does Mr. Precooked Pot Roast or Spaghetti use a cookbook, ever? The killer: EW announces that she will buy a new sink stopper. Will pay for it herself (not a gift). Puts the 20+ year old still perfectly good because it works stopper into a plastic grocery *bag, wondering if she'll need it for sizing, and goes to Home Depot. $2.00 item. The helper man takes a look at it and its rotting rubber bottom and food on it and finds the replacement. EW, with chagrin, says she's buying it for "my boyfriend." Home Depot guy says that such a good woman deserves special attention and thanks – massage, hotel room, etc. She considers throwing it away but then keeps it, just in case Steve still wants it. EW jokes that he may want some of it for lunch.*

"I'm still waiting for a valid argument," says Steve.

Steve's first date: 13-year-old boy takes a girl he has a crush on to the movies. He does the perfunctory yawn, reaching around to her opposite shoulder with his arm. He thinks he's incredibly smooth; she didn't even notice. His hand is 2" away from her breast. He's 2 inches away from first base, how great is that? They are watching "War and Peace," a four-hour movie, and he is afraid to move his arm lest he lose ground. The arm and hand are tingling, but he grits it out. "Do you think that she wanted you to touch her breast?" "I don't know, 13 year old boys are nonverbal so of course I wouldn't have asked. She wasn't writhing or moaning or anything."

Freedom, i.e. #1 on Relationship Wish List

EW doesn't fail to remind him that he can walk.

Mars/Venus & dousing of water during dog wash

Note: EW's head was down, Steve was oblivious that he was being obnoxious by just commenting on the dog's disgruntlement w/ the bath. Steve couldn't see EW's eyes to read the situation better. EW's getting pissed that (once again) she is doing all of the work. She's washing, rinsing and periodically capturing the dog, while he's standing around making wisecracks, She stands up, holding the basin of water, looking at him, weighing what to do. She doesn't tell him that he needs to stop and help, or that she's unhappy. A pregnant moment, and then SLOSH, she throws the entire basin at him, dousing him from head to sneakers. Actually it was the basinful minus about 5 cups of water, plus 14 dog hairs.

Who will tell Paul first?

WE.

What does that mean. Do I really have a boyfriend, he have a girl-friend, for public purposes? He's been alone for over 10 years. She has been less-than-respectfully treated for nearly 20. Why want WE?

Mutuality, sensuousness.

Is there such a thing as satisfying, pre-orgasmic sex? 90% is the code word.

How to decipher what is good, what works for both parties, the guy and the girl, at this stage in life? What's the physiological component of satisfaction, does it have to be ejaculation? Or the involuntary Kegeling for a woman? What about the psychological barriers we construct in self-defense, and deconstruct when we feel safe?

Need to inquire of medical specialist about 4X, how the prostate figures in sex. Don't know. Does 4X interfere with normal orgasm?

What about my role? I try to make anything enjoyable perfectly safe. Anything safe perfectly enjoyable. Am I trying to transfer my preferences, my qualities, over to the male? Is that possible?

How about when we're having intercourse and I think I'm offering encouragement, "Go!" What if that puts pressure, deflationary pressure on Laz? It's true that our best intentions can easily backfire, especially in long-standing relationships. Not unlike our siblings, an intake of breath can be misinterpreted and send the entire communication in the wrong direction.

Does Afib affect how long/hard an erection is?

Erection issues:
1. pill, Viagra, enabling 60+ males to continue with their conception of virility, and perhaps what satisfies a woman, "wham-bam." Barbie-women, homogenization of our culture to expect men to have an orgasm every time. Does Viagra perpetuate the male, sexist view of sex? Do women actually want it this way – he comes and then falls asleep?
2. maybe nature doesn't intend it to be that way.
3. other option would be softer, longer, lingering play, which would enable aging sex to take advantage of sensuality, intimacy that a woman craves. What can a male learn about pleasure from women? I.E., if he doesn't have an orgasm, which undercuts a woman's pleasure. A woman doesn't need their male to have an orgasm to enhance her pleasure.

Example, Steve is not an insensitive male; he understands need for talk in order to learn.

(Roofer.)

How do men evolve, if possible, from the proverbial teenager with a perpetual hard-on, into the more sensitive male (SM)? Understanding that male physiology includes a "sleeping pill" in their orgasm.

Would this be a story and a guide to how to help your man evolve, to learn about prolonged pleasure? With Jerque, he's awake and available to continue.

Women, this woman, found it psychologically diminishing to be never receiving at least a little attention. If one has to ask, then this underscores the fact that it didn't occur to one's partner that you are a person there, you are someone who cares about their needs and pleasure and satisfaction, but then it didn't occur to him that you are still there, waiting and hoping, when they are finished. Sex could become gross, except that I was constantly trying to make it safe for him. I guess I knew enough to accept his limits and try to help him along. Instead, I became just used. That feels lousy. As I read this, I feel the tingles of pain, all over my body. My shoulders slump forward. I lower my gaze. Is it worse to be raped or to consensually give over one's body again and again?

WHAT DOES CONSENT AND SENSUAL HAVE IN COMMON? Nothing, in the above case. Yuk. It's very damaging. I made a choice and lost a lot. I can't say that I lost a chance to have a real marriage with real love, because I don't know how I would have behaved differently with another. But I did lose a lot of time. Got bullied from nearly the beginning.

For my children, may they enjoy and share a lifetime of rich, mutual caring and understanding with those who value them.

transcendental

Do you ever wonder about a religion
Embracing faith as the only key to heaven
Though contrary to the reason you were given
Since faith transcends the limits of rational men?

Has your reason actually been transcended
Or as a matter of fact simply suspended?

hedging Bets

Some believers in Christianity
See faith as the key to their destiny
Opening the gates to eternity.

And if it turns out that they are all wrong
No real harm for having just gone along.
Whereas non-believers lose either way
And may have the devil to pay someday.

As if an omniscient deity
Would not see through such blatant sophistry.

Chapter 8
FINANCING COLLEGE

My motivation to excel in school was reinforced by my mother, and also by my public school teachers. The explicit goal was a college education. The mantra repeated daily: "If you want to get into college, you must (fill in the blank): study hard, get good grades, pay attention, complete homework, behave, etc." Since these were the Sputnik years, another constant refrain emphasized science courses: "If you want to go to college, you must take algebra, chemistry, geometry, trigonometry and calculus." Struggling to get A's in these difficult science courses probably helped, but a course in introductory Spanish would have served me much better in college and later life. Unfortunately, no one ever said: "If you want to get a college degree, you should learn a foreign language." Spanish was an elective offered by my public high school, but only a few of my classmates signed up.

College always seemed a remote possibility for me since my mother struggled just to put food on the table for her five children. One day when I was about fifteen years old, Ollie Prindle, the Republican banker who gave me a summer job in his bank, called me into his office.

"Steve, several of my friends and I, who want to remain anonymous, have been impressed by all your good work, and we want you to know that we will make sure you have the funds needed for college."

I was in shock and fighting tears of joy as I left his office. I would be able to go to college after all. To this day I remember with gratitude the sense of community and mutual support thriving in a small town in Michigan, and hopefully in similar communities across our country. Ollie Prindle and his business colleagues on Main Street lived by a different set of values than the greedheads on Wall Street, who in their relentless pursuit of personal gain, benefit from the winner-take-all economy that today threatens the very social fabric that ties us together as a nation. Ollie, who became my mentor in the absence of a father, represented the best of a Republican Party that has lost its way. Our political views may have differed (he advised a "my country, right or wrong" approach when I was agonizing over how to respond to the Vietnam War draft), but, like David Brooks today, no one ever doubted his fundamental decency.

Ollie's fundamental decency extended to his wife, Jean, and their children. Although we were at opposite ends of the SES (socio-economic status) spectrum, my siblings played with their children as if there were no SES gap. Our small town did not have the larger SES conflicts between minorities found in larger cities; the primary difference was white SES and it was substantial and played out with difficulty in some parts of town. But not with Ollie and Jean and most of the town. I especially appreciated the fact that Ollie and Jean always treated my mother with respect. I hope it's still that way in small towns across America. I haven't seen much evidence of it in larger cities and suburbs, probably due to the fact that there is little interaction among SES classes to begin with as more and more Americans opt for gated communities and other isolated homogeneous enclaves. Perhaps important exceptions can be found in some employer-employee settings, churches and other community organizations.

I studied hard and earned my A's the hard way. When our class of about one hundred and fifty graduated, I was one of ten Distinguished Honor Students. One teacher told me confidentially that a female classmate and I were tied for highest grade point average, but she had not taken the difficult science courses. So I was as competitive in the classroom as I was on the basketball court, and, excelling at both, many colleges offered scholarships.

The University of Michigan seemed most attractive: Big Ten Conference for Division 1 competition, and excellent secular education. Then a postcard from a Harvard alumnus arrived in the mail: "Dear Steve, *The Lansing State Journal* reports that you have been named to the All-State Basketball team, and are a straight A student. Have you thought about going to Harvard?" —Don Peters

Harvard? Wasn't that one of those expensive Ivy League schools that catered to rich preppies? No, of course I had never thought about going to Harvard, but I replied with a short note: "Dear Mr. Peters: Thank you for your interest, but I cannot afford to go to an expensive school like Harvard." Shortly thereafter a second postcard from Peters: "Dear Steve, don't worry about the expense. Harvard will provide a scholarship and financial aid if they want you. Have you taken the SAT?"

Three weeks later, without any specific preparation, I took the SAT. Then I completed the Harvard application and soon was on a bus to Lansing for an interview with another Harvard alumnus. Ricardo Voigt was a judge of some sort, but I never asked, being somewhat overwhelmed by the setting in a fancy restaurant high up in a Lansing skyscraper. I had only eaten in a restaurant a few times, and never one with white linen tablecloths. I was nervous, and afraid that I might use the wrong fork or spill my food.

Judge Voigt, "What's the matter Steve, don't you like the food?"

Steve, "No sir, the food is very good. I guess I'm a bit nervous. I've never appeared before a Judge before. I mean I've never talked with a Judge before."

Judge Voigt laughed, and after that the interview seemed to go well, although I was not sure because he appeared to nod off several times. At the end of the interview the Judge asked me if I had any questions.

Steve, "Just one. The University of Michigan has offered me a full-ride scholarship, but when I asked the coach what would happen if I broke a leg or otherwise couldn't play, he said they would then have to give the scholarship to someone who could. What is Harvard's policy?"

Judge Voigt, "Harvard does not have athletic scholarships, and doesn't care if you play or not. Just pass your courses, and keep your nose clean."

Steve, "I think I can manage that. I've always been a good student, and I'm not afraid of hard work."

Judge Voigt, "I usually don't say this, Steve, but don't worry. I'm going to give you a good recommendation."

Several weeks later the third postcard from Peters, "Dear Steve, Congratulations. Your college boards hit at 600 or better, and Harvard will be offering you a full scholarship. Official letter from Harvard will arrive in about one week or less." I was stunned and near tears once again, remembering Ollie Prindle's businessmen who several years earlier had quietly and generously offered to pay for my college education. I would not need it now, but I never forgot this remarkable offer, and what America could be if not for the greedheads. I folded the postcard to fit into my wallet, and for days afterwards would re-read it frequently to make sure I was not dreaming. This poor boy was going to Harvard!

Almost everyone in our small town was surprised and supportive upon hearing of my Harvard admission. The first boy from the small town ever to get into Harvard was a big deal, but how could a poor boy afford such an expensive school? Speculation can get out of hand in a small town:

The Editor's Corner.....CONGRATULATIONS, STEVE

It has been a pleasure for the newspaper to chronicle this outstanding young man's accomplishments and the latest announcement has been the most satisfying of all....It will be interesting to see what notable achievement is next linked with Steve's name. Considering his brilliant mind, his strong body, his insatiable craving for knowledge and his intense desire to excel, there is seemingly no limit to his potential.

My God, how does one live up to that? I just don't want to be the first to flunk out of Harvard. Is there a place for a poor boy at Harvard?

take time

Take the time, they say, do not delay
To smell the flowers along the way
Because we have only day-to-day
Do not hurry your whole life away.

No matter what your boss or friends may say
Save some hours for flowers every day
And let's take time before time takes us
To enjoy, reflect and be generous.

On knowing

Some divide religious philosophy
Into believers in eternity
And atheistic negativity
And yet they are so very much alike
In being positively sure they're right
And in knowing that they know they know
Although the real division one can show
Is between their absolute certitude
And all those who have been forced to conclude
That life does elude such exactitude
And remains immersed within mysteries
Beyond reach of our ideologies.
Therefore not knowing isn't just politic
But the logic for turning agnostic.

Chapter 9
LIZ'S NOTES AND SILVER PANSY

Intro: Steve	
Intro/Chapter 1: Eliza	
Relationship Wish List: Steve	Includes explanation of why #6 is 6th. 10 years ago was last sex. Ain't looking because it's been so long and doesn't know if the equipment works.
RWL: Eliza	Comments on Steve's RWL. Early vs. Late love and what drives us all to sex. My RWL, from my female and older w/ family point of view. Where I'm coming from, N – XXX years.

Our First Time:

Steve, perpetual hard on, undistracted except for perhaps nuclear explosion.

Eliza, first time, second time "I did that already."

Family History:

Steve, never married, marriage-phobe, does not have any inclination to have children, perpetuate his name. Sees the institution as only important for raising children. Otherwise not interested. He has plenty of siblings who are populating the world. A good relationship is a good relationship, doesn't need marriage for the convention of it.

Segue to: Our parents' marriages, and what we learned and didn't learn from them.

How EW got married.

Contrast EW's marriage vs. SM's bachelorhood:
Dependency? Opportunities? Privilege vs. poor

Sex: Different for females vs. males.

A woman can fake an orgasm. (WHY??)A man can't fake, i.e. he needs to have an erection; it's not a measure of ejaculation/orgasm.

Female: Is she ready? She can have a decent relationship w/o orgasm but a male can't w/o an erection. That's what sells Viagra.

Irony:

Males have a perpetual hard on during teen years, insatiable. But in later years, has a woman who enjoys sex as much as he, and wants to be w/ him, finally. A dream woman, but what's going on with Laz?

Or, when you're old enough to have XXX to burn, then the fire has gone out.

EW encourages – don't need for male to come/orgasm in order to satisfy a woman, in fact it can be even better for her because there's less stress about completion. "We'll try again later, who cares?" It's just between you and me and I'm fine and happy w/ your caresses and company.

I versus We: last chapter.

I'm here at a hot springs resort with a guy. A guy? What does that mean? Come on, Eliza, you know what a guy is, what aren't you saying? He's feeding me bakery bread dipped in delicious pickle juice, for breakfast. It is truly tasty cinnamon fruit bread, baked yesterday at a small town bakery we stopped at en route here, but the jar of pickles was a gift from a friend and came from his home county in Ohio.

Steve is more than 'a guy' to me.

So what is he? That's why we're writing this. What and who are the both of us at this later time in our lives? It's about what we are, and what we aren't, and what really matters now.

We discussed the usual terminology the other day: boyfriend, lover, *just someone from our alumni club.* To me, 'boyfriend' seems to be a label applied to a high school infatuation. Nowadays, high school kids hang out together and hook up, without becoming very attached emotionally to each other. They are much better at being friends with each other than Steve or I ever was. The definition of sexual attachment used to begin with explicit or implicit exclusive access.

As for what defined Steve's high school relationship(s) in the 60's, I'll leave that for him to relate. I spent my high school years at an all-girls school which may have seemed to have a religious affiliation but didn't. That doesn't mean that we didn't feel cloistered from boys. We complained as all teenage girls are apt to do, but no one seems to be regretful or scarred from the experience.

The single sex school experience didn't bother me. I was bookish and studied hard and wanted to go to a good college. We all knew that boys, uh, matured at a different rate. I mean, doh, so there was no great loss that there weren't boys around.

I did go out on one date during my three years there. It also was my first kiss. What a shock it was to have him slip his tongue into my mouth. Gross. You'd think that a nest of teenage girls would have little else to talk about but boys, especially educating each other and anticipating these rites of passage. Most of my peers were more experienced than I.

Now I'm in my (early) 50's and aware of the difference between words and experience, the gray area of interpretation of truth and delighted to see this as a lifelong process. Hopefully, I'm nearing a point where I can use whatever wisdom I may have accumulated over these years to be productive and helpful.

Notes: The list, gender differences, sex and more sex

Today's youth and hooking up, freer sex without consequences or attachment. Grace getting asked for "road head" in the hallway at school, just two days after she had her first kiss with him.

Sex: Women of the 70's, Bill Clinton's very public defense that oral sex is not sex. Steve thinking that oral sex is much more intimate than intercourse. Long ago, the 'duty' oral sex, i.e. for a birthday present will suffer with administering it on the partner's birthday. Steve and Liz both enjoy it, terrific intimacy with another facet of pleasure. Why? Because we can and do talk about it; what works, what doesn't (without fear of rejecting or rejection); more interesting, intimate and mutual.

At this stage in my life, I'm more comfortable with my body, WYSIWYG; what you see is what you get. Kids of today think hooking up is very casual, friends with privileges.

Since the 80's and the advent of AIDS, STDs are so rampant; there was a small window between the freedom of having the pill, i.e. not being concerned about becoming pregnant or parents and then the STD 'epidemic' (EW words).

Number Six: Whereas Liz read it as "Wants to have sex with ME," emphasis on his need to find someone who singularly wants him for his obvious attributes. ME versus someone or anyone else; ME capitalized because it's a self-centered way of expressing that he is the center of the sexual experience.

Steve's true expression of #6, thought out extremely carefully to be mutual, and definitely NOT self-centered, and he thought this wording through very carefully as he composed it, and he was very pleased that he had written it very mutually. "I'm baffled, astounded that you would think that something I worded so carefully, made numerous edits and really revised carefully and then you read it in a totally different way. My, how does that happen? How can we be so off?"

We later exchanged an e-mail called *The Black Bra*. Liz saw it this way; Steve that way.

Therein lies the issue. With enough time, caring and patience, we can work it out. Sounds like a phrase borrowed from a Beatles tune, but it seems to be apt.

How do we get there? Not trying to fulfill a checklist or any one else's expectation. If something goes awry, we talk, fix, learn or come to the conclusion that we're off and will solve it later. My black and white years are behind me. Treat people with respect, learn about them and decide if you have enough time or need in your life to keep that relationship current. Family? Always. Ex-husband? Keep it civil, respectful. Don't pretend that you don't need to talk sometimes. Lying by omission (choosing not to give some detail) is still lying. Or is it?

"Love is giving the benefit of the doubt," and so if one person recognizes that there is misunderstanding or talking on two different tracks, we'll go back and dig and define and get back on track/purpose.

"We can work it out," recognize that there is some issue misunderstood, have faith that you both can resolve it, applies to small and big things. We're doing the best with the knowledge, tools, information that we have. We will work it out, defined by this difference, there's no impending loss or shame.

Silver Pansy

On the way to Mount Princeton Hot Springs Resort with Liz for a long weekend, I suggested we stop in Silver Plume for breakfast. The blue collar Silver Plume (population 169, down from about 2,000 in 1885) is connected to its wealthier upscale neighbor Georgetown (population about 1,000) two miles down the mountain by Interstate I-70. It's twice as far by the famous Georgetown Loop Railroad, an engineering marvel which once was Colorado's main tourist attraction. Steam locomotives still puff and twist their way on three-foot narrow gauge rail in the narrow Clear Creek Canyon between the two towns.

Pulling off Interstate 70 at the Silver Plume exit one immediately notices the unpaved roads and small barely-embellished Victorian dwellings, many seemingly abandoned. The nineteenth century Main Street completes the picture of a Hollywood ghost town, but it is not, as over 100 hardy souls live here year round. Turning west on Main Street, marked at the corner by a vintage Colorado & Southern caboose next to a white frame City Hall, one soon comes to a magnificent brick Victorian schoolhouse (now turned into a museum). You have to be impressed by how much these struggling miners and merchants living in modest frame houses in Silver Plume must have valued education to build such an impressive building. The frame church on Main Street, on the other hand, is relatively modest in scale and appearance.

Years ago I was so charmed by Silver Plume that I bought a small Victorian house across Clear Creek from the bandstand on Main Street. I thought it a good investment in a mountain house that I could rent, and occasionally occupy during the summer. The idea was better than the reality as the bitterly cold winters and difficulty with normal repairs soon dampened my enthusiasm. Yet I still like to stop in Silver Plume every time I pass by. A few years ago on the way to a reunion in Telluride, I suggested to Paul K. Bryant and Jeff Horney that we stop for breakfast at the Silver Plume Antique Shop and Tea Room. The tea room is located in a nineteenth century frame building across the unpaved street from Ted Parker's K&P Hall General Store where I once bought a unique carved antique Italian bookcase more appropriate for a fine antique shop in tony Georgetown two miles away. Look closely at the detail in the photos on the following pages and you will see the Putto flipping the bird at passersby. The smaller putti on both sides of the glass doors similarly sport middle finger salutes. While we waited for our scrambled eggs and toast in the combination antique shop and cafe, Jeff Horney, looking like Jerry Garcia from The Grateful Dead, entertained us with an accomplished rendition of a Chopin concerto on the grand piano next to our table. It was a special breakfast in a nineteenth century setting that we'll long remember.

Putti Bookcase

*Putti
Bookcase
Detail
(above)*

*Putti
Bookcase
Books
(to left)*

So repeat the scene with Liz, only this time our attention is drawn to an oil painting of an attractive female nude on the wall behind the piano. The typed description to one side, "This oil painting hung in the Jolly Roger Roadhouse (Bar), located on Lake City Way, north of Seattle. The roadhouse was built in the early 30's. It was torn down in the 1970's. We purchased it in Edmonds, Washington. The painting is by J. W. Duckworth, 1933." Liz and I both liked the painting, but it seemed a bit pricey for a bar nude by what probably was an unlisted artist. With the owner's permission, we took each other's SEG (shit-eating grin) photo with the nude. Liz also snapped a smart-phone picture without contemporary company. After an egg salad sandwich and tea, we purchased a loaf of fresh baked bread at a Victorian bakery a few steps away, and a friend at the old Buckley Store gave us a jar of Ohio Amish pickles to take with us to Mount Princeton.

The weekend was great fun. We arrived too late the first night for the resort's dinner, so we dined on Silver Plume bread dipped in Ohio pickle sauce on the king-size bed in our room facing white chalk cliffs. It was an unexpected and delicious meal, and so was the TNT (touch and talk) about late love and childhood memories that carried us through the night until sunrise. Neither of us was tired, but after a brief nap we played some tennis, and Liz convinced me against my better judgment to try the giant waterslide next to the tennis courts. It was one of those moments frequently experienced with Liz where something I was reluctant to do turned into something fun and memorable. Liz couldn't stop laughing at my less than elegant splash from waterslide into pool with, as she put it, my size fourteens flailing high above my head prior to a spectacular back flop into the water. We were brave enough to take the slide together, in an upright spoonary position, which was stimulating for different reasons. Back on the patio outside our room Liz wrote her first chapter of *Metaphors'* late love issues and reflections. I am impressed with the compelling voice of her well-written first chapter – one that should contrast nicely with my first chapter and introduction.

Late that afternoon Liz and I drove to the little art town of Salida where we enjoyed burrito steak dinners on The Boathouse restaurant deck while watching kids below us tube and kayak down the Arkansas River rapids. That night our sexual play continued unabated, except we relaxed long enough to discuss the Silver Plume painting. We joked about a name for the nude, and decided on Silver Pansy. Silver for Silver Plume, and Pansy for an aunt whose full-bodied figure reminded Liz of the nude in the oil painting. We decided to make an offer on the painting, and buy it jointly (a first!), which we would then alternate hanging in her house and my house. On the way back to Boulder we stopped in historic Leadville, home of the legendary Baby Doe Tabor and her Matchless Mine, which was celebrating its annual Boom Days, an ironic name given the town's long history of hard times. I made the call to Silver Plume with our offer on the painting, explaining that we had checked the internet and could find no listing for J. W. Duckworth that might make the painting valuable. The owner, however, refused to negotiate, so Liz later made poster size blow-ups of the photo she had taken of Silver Pansy, and thus we each had one to frame and remind us of our memorable trip into the Colorado mountains.

I could not stop thinking about the original each time I saw the blow-up photo of Silver Pansy, now nicely framed in my family room and another in Liz's bedroom, and so at one point I decided to give myself a birthday present. I paid full price for Silver Pansy. And now, dear Reader, you too can enjoy Silver Pansy, at least indirectly. She graces the cover of all three volumes of *Metaphors: A Reverse Love Story*.

Silver Pansy

brawl games

It was not so many seasons ago
That to the boxing ring all fans would go
To cheer and jeer the fighters blow by blow
And hear the punches land from the first row.

Then ice skaters started to skate amuck
Fists and sticks flew more often than the puck
To hit or get hit with a hockey stick
Is cheered far more than turning a hat trick.

Without real reprimand soon fan demand
Helped these battles expand across sport land.
If you watch footbrawl you know it is true
You saw more action after whistles blew.

When "left hook" is the commentator's call
We stop and listen with rapt attention
Not sure in today's game of basketbrawl
If he meant to the hoop or to the chin.

Of course basebrawl is not to be outdone
Heads are hit as often as a home run.
Have you seen anyone get hit with a bat?
If not already, it may come to that.

With brawl games now wired for sound effect
Moans and groans players practice to perfect
You hear them cuss and fuss and swear and scream
And might even think they are really mean.

Three cheers for today's professional brawl
It may even be the fan's last windfall
Since you needn't pay more for this addition
All's included in the price of admission.

Please don't think me mentally deficient
For pointing out a plus we shouldn't ignore
These brave young men will be so proficient
If our country must fight another war.

Chapter 10
MISCELLANEOUS E-MAILS

Hi Pack!

Yes, keep writing. Miss you too. Hope we can re-connect sometime soon.

Hugs,

Steve

Hi Steve,

So last night, I brought forth so many images from our waking in the morning. I looked at your eyes from below, again. Felt your right arm around my shoulder and draped across my chest while we're lying on our sides, spooned. Ran my nails down the last bit of your forearm, checked out the breadth of your wrist and texture of the hair there, scrolled my fingers down yours. Heard your rumbling tones in my left ear. I felt much more comfort after that exercise. I pushed my backside against the curve of your groin and ran my left hand all over your hip. Your skin is so smooth there. It's a restorative exercise. I hope you're having a sweet morning yourself.

With love,

Liz

Liz,

Among other things, I like the way you think.

Steve

Steve,

That's very kind of you. I've been lying in bed, thinking about us and what we have that's comforting and also wondering why I can't conjure up how I see you after you roll over after lovemaking. It must be because I have my eyes closed, taking in the feel of you and have let go of any need for visual confirmation. I decided that was ok. So, sleep well and know that your Pack was fondling these thoughts of you.

Liz

Subject: Skeptics
Paul,

Great to see you again. You mentioned the Big Sur skeptics conference to which Les invited you and Janet. You and Les may enjoy a book I am currently reading, "The Doubter's Companion: A Dictionary of Aggressive Common Sense" by John Ralston Saul. He's the Canadian skeptic best known for "Voltaire's Bastards". Examples:

UNIVERSITY: A place in which civilization's knowledge is divided up into exclusive territories.

ASPEN INSTITUTE: A supermarket of conventional wisdom for middle-level executives.

WISDOM: The purpose of doubt. Wisdom, then is life with uncertainty, the opposite of power or ideology.

Liz and I are looking forward to seeing you again at your wedding, if not before.

Steve

Subject: Update
Good morning Liz,

Hope your back is better by the time you read this. Is another preventive trip to the doc in order?

Enjoyed your surprise visit yesterday morning, and part II of the "Spring" movie. I keep pondering various scenes and think it is one of the best movies ever, with themes of greed, home, provincial attitudes, love, revenge, regret, generations, unintended consequences, etc. We agree that the mark of a good movie is making one think, so another great choice – and more to come!

Hugs,

Steve

Hi Liz,

Here is a draft of the possible lead-in I mentioned for "Reverse Love Story." Feel free to revise and/or start from scratch. Or simply ignore and delete as there is no pressure and we can jettison this project at any time. I set this up as us writing alternate chapters from our different perspectives, but if we go forward we may want to try to integrate our perspectives in a double-helix form where our perspectives emerge naturally as part of pillow talk or other exchanges. For example, our different backgrounds could emerge as we tell each other over time about our families, history, etc. as part of getting to know each other. Also, I used real names thinking we could substitute fictitious ones later, but perhaps if we started with fictitious names and places we would feel like we have more poetic license to create a more interesting story (less biographical, more novel). What do you think?

Hugs,

Steve

Subject: List for You

Hey Steve,

I started by copying all of our notes. At the end there, I was journaling pain. You don't have to get involved with that.

Many hugs,

Liz

Subject: List for You

Yes, Liz, this is a great start. I was laughing again at some of the exchanges between Liz and Steve, which also raise substantive issues of probable interest to boomers. An example is the "four steps behind" metaphor, which if elaborated on with related themes such as mutuality and obliviousness, could be a chapter in itself. The key of course, as you indicate, is how these notes get organized into readable chapters or other context. Do we try to put the discussion into conversational exchanges (pillow talk) within a chapter (with different perceptions of same event like dog wash, number six semantics, etc. or contrast between backgrounds, family, etc.) in double helix mode or past tense reflections by each in alternate chapters? Perhaps easier to start with alternate chapters. I am impressed that you wrote this much within such a short window when you were in yawn girl recovery mode from migraine. Are you ready to take a run at a first chapter following my introduction, or prefer to continue with random listing of other issues and exchanges as basis for later organization into chapters? Or just write on and see what develops? This is fun. I will look through our e-mail exchanges to try to identify some that could be incorporated whole into the book (like wish list) and used as a basis for further comment. Looking forward to further discussions and drafts.

Hugs,

Steve

Subject: Inside Job

Paul,

Liz and I just saw "Inside Job" and highly recommend it in part as additional support for The Civic Standard and critical thinking in general. We agree with Marshall Fine's fine conclusion:

"Inside Job" should be required viewing for all citizens. Instead, it's destined to be one of those movies that critics rave about and people who already know this material go to see. But it should be shown in every college and high school in all the economics, civics or social studies classes in America, to inform a generation that might, possibly, recognize our essentially greedy human nature and figure out how to learn from past mistakes.

If this is too dark, follow it up with "The Social Network," which we also enjoyed.

(I'll recommend my mother's egg nog: 2 parts egg nog mix, 1 part dark rum, ½ part brandy and float 2 parts vanilla ice cream in it until melted. Goes down rather smoothly.)

Happy Holidays,
Steve and Liz

Subject: Male men
Dear Pack,

I am dreaming of Bermuda and you beating the heat by walking Singing Beach. Both good memories.

After my swim today I was on the porch reading one of the books I purchased yesterday, Jim Harrison's "The English Major" and LOL at page 98:

English Major, "I was thrown off balance by this young woman. I mean forty-three but that's maybe too young for me."

Son, "Dad, even in my world you can't SKIP two generations...she said you often cry and refuse affection."

English Major, "She wore my pecker to a frazzle. I had to buy steroid ointment."

Son, "Dad, there are dozens of effective lubricants on the market. Just BUY some old-fashioned Corn Huskers."

I was still laughing when I saw the new mailman (my regular mailman is having foot surgery today) try to deliver my mail by the side entrance to the backyard. He apologized when he realized his mistake. I said, "No problem, it happened once before."

So you are very much in my thoughts, dear Liz, and this is only part of it. I hesitate to revisit these memories, but consider it payback for laughing at me wrestling with my pillow – and losing!

Hugs,

Steve

Subject: Male Men

Steve,

My goodness, this is a very intimate letter! Starting with the pecker frazzling and then linking us with the Corn Huskers, side entrance and pillow fight. Since now we've been apart for so long, am I going to be shy when I see you? How will we reacquaint? I'm quite certain I'll listen to myself and know what to do – so was it a fair question? I have an envelope for you that got stuck in my bag during transition time.

So dear Steve, let's start anew. A demain.

Liz

Subject: Metaphors – Ending

Liz,

Can't sleep as some ideas for "Metaphors'" ending keep turning in my head and want to record them before I forget.

We talked about reverse love story tear jerk ending where it is the poor girl who dies early with the rich boy by her bedside. So reverse where poor midwestern boy dies early with rich Boston girl by his bedside.

Their relationship also never gets a chance to mature, as a stroke caused by his Afib paralyzes him from head down. He still has some quality of life, as only one of his brains is useless. He can still listen to music, watch TV and talk but not touch. But he is no Stephen Hawkings who can endure in this condition. He wants Liz to pull his plug. He cannot adjust to his new condition after a lifetime of athleticism and renewed sexuality. He points out the irony that he was always worried Liz would dump him because of the age gap, but now he wants her to dump him (reason 103 for love and granting him his last wish, not contemplated in the original wish list). He thought he had achieved the perfect balance with the perfect package, Liz – but now his number one goal of freedom is impossible as he is trapped inside of a prison with his paralyzed body. He wants Liz to pull the plug so he once again is free, even if not with her. She also knows he means it when he says that he wants her to find a new guy to share her life with. She has too much sexual vitality to sacrifice herself to a paralyzed body. She has already sacrificed a good part of her life to a loveless marriage to protect her children. But Steve does not want to live to see her find new late love with some other guy. Steve cannot stand the thought that she will now sacrifice her life to tending to his useless body. He wants her to dump him by pulling the plug and giving them both number one, freedom. The docs will not agree to pulling the plug given Steve's functioning head senses, and it would be illegal to do so. There is a living will but it does not deal with this question since it only talks about Do Not Revive if…

Liz's dilemma is compounded by the fact that she is more spiritual than he and remnants of her Catholic schoolgirl background surface and pulling the plug is taboo. They discuss and debate the great religious issues. He says that he agrees with Hitchens and Dawkins that religion is Santa Claus for adults and that God is that ever shrinking part of life that science cannot explain. Knowledge versus faith, etc. She sees the hand of God in everything; he thinks this is soft thinking for the weak who need such consolation and false belief. He reminds her that his exclamation about meeting Liz and then Liz's role in reviving Laz (thank you God, I am now a believer) was truly a joke and not a real conversion. He begs Liz to give him one last gift; number one, freedom. Everything about her personal morality and religion and self-protection tells her not to do it, but after much mental anguish she, out of love, pulls the plug and grants Steve his final freedom. She walks away from the hospital and the readers from the book, with a handkerchief to wipe away the tears.

What do you think?
Steve

Subject: Metaphors – Ending
Steve,

This is superb! The angst is extremely palpable. We'll talk. I'm so sad I can't swallow.
Liz

Lady From Wisconsin

Her friends often called her two-plate Pat
And she was very, very proud of that
This creative lady from Wisconsin
Who bought a small house in Boulderton
For her antique country furniture
And exquisite hand-made miniatures.
When suddenly it occurred to her
To create in one room a crazy corner
With items to be bought at garage sale
Since no longer available at retail.

First came a plastic Garfield the cat tent
So confident it would be magnificent
Proving her taste was somewhat different.
And then for Garfield the cat's nourishment
A plastic wiener from Oscar Meyer
That could not tempt any other buyer.
Since it had a small leak, the sales lady
Could hardly speak, and unloaded it for free.
For Garfield's other paw it was evident
A Budweiser beer tin was imminent.

Although it was overpriced at a dime
For the crazy corner, it was sublime.

She bought a grass skirt to adorn her
But nobody who saw dared to warn her
As the grass did not extend from end to end
The effect is quite shocking to comprehend.
Next came a green/orange carrot windsock
Sure to be the only one on any block.
Then she purchased a card-playing dog rug,
And a large chicken-footed drinking mug.
And other treasures of equal allure
She bought with limited expenditure.

You could get the complete listing from her
But I'm sure you're now getting the picture.
In fact, she got so very carried away
When it finally came to moving day
She squeezed in her hand-made miniatures
But there was no room for the furniture,
And the artistic lady from Wisconsin
Found neither she nor her antiques could get in.

Chapter 11
STEVE'S JOURNALS

utuality

6/21/10. I am finding my new life with Liz so special, but often when I try to relive the experience, I realize that I forget the key parts experienced only a few days before. Paul says, "nouns go first," and I find that true for me as well, along with details of our evolving relationship. Therefore even though I have to force myself to do so, I have started to journal our experiences. Sometimes when I do so, I get on a roll and record in great detail. Here is a sample from three days of such writing:

As my 68th birthday is imminent, I reflect on the reverse love story that Liz and I embarked on four months ago. I think we are somewhat unique in finding a new level of passion at our advanced ages that is based on mutuality rather than the slam-bam thank-you-ma'am unverbal sex of teenage love. But Liz brings by a *NY Times* article yesterday about sexuality in preteen girls that talks about the window after the pill and before AIDs when sex enjoyed some halcyon days (the 70's when Liz also first explored her sexuality), and some of the guys who took the journey of mutuality rather than conquest with them.

One lesson of our mutuality journey for me has been the pleasure I receive and give when I am semi-erect and/or non-orgasmic during sex. I keep wanting to reach orgasm as a way of proving my manhood or achieving ultimate release or something. Liz keeps repeating that such is not necessary to enjoying our sexual experience, and in fact is better since it enables more and longer sexual play; and time for her to build up to eventual orgasm. She reached orgasm with me in Los Angeles for the first time in years and started to cry with joy. I should have stayed with the manual play that got her there rather than moving on to other new experiences like a lotion substitute for vaseline, and jokes about the Husker's corn oil that she had given Jeffrey the roofer for his chapped hands.

The other night she was crying again after I extended my manual exploration of Bermuda. I felt her tears on my face after one episode, but had earlier turned out the lights. I need at least a dim light to see her face and grimaces to help me find the button and right touch since just moans and groans are often not enough. So I explain this to Liz, and we discuss lighting at night, which does not bother her, both in my bedroom with the dimmer switch, and her bedroom with closet light or alternatives since the digital clock light is inadequate.

Liz went to *Vagina Monologues* at the Denver Performing Arts Center (DPAC) with neighbor Audrey, and then came by my house after the play about 10:30 p.m. We went directly to bed, but I had not seen Liz for two weekends of custody and getting reacquainted took much longer than jumping naked into bed again. The experience was pleasant but not as charged as usual, but then the next morning after sleeping the night naked and spooned together I felt our bodies had melted together and we had some delicious love making, including what Liz later described as my "bowling ball control of Bermuda." Another great metaphor from Liz once again since that is exactly what it seemed like with one of my fingers in her B-hole (Bermuda), one on B2 (B-squared, her button), and a third up her A-hole (butt-hole). A good metaphor in one sense in the three-finger analogy, but so opposite the hard and cold feel of a bowling ball in another. Talking about this kind of metaphor with Liz later, where something is both like and unlike at the same time, I relate the children's story of the king who would reward his kingdom's riches to the citizen who could deliver him something to eat that was both hot and cold at the same time. All failed, except for one peasant who won the riches by creating a hot-fudge sundae for the king.

I had backed off the anal experience since Los Angeles as I was not sure Liz wanted to continue after our LA exploration, but Thursday morning as I was lightly stroking her body I noticed her writhing and moaning as I touched above and near her A-hole and increased moaning and shifting that helped me move directly to target and then to vaseline which Liz passed to me from the counter next to my bed. And so the bowling ball metaphor.

6/22/10. Following Colvin's "determined practice," Liz and I met at the middle school tennis courts near my house this morning about 8 a.m. before it got too hot to play and hit tennis balls, using the new system we devised whereby one of us is always at the net blocking shots back to the other. This improves ball control and increases the number of swings and practice. We switch when all the balls of the net person are behind him or her. Also, we use twelve or more balls so we are spending more time hitting rather than chasing and picking up balls. I comment that this morning we are both hitting stronger and more consistently than ever and mention our version of determined practice. Liz quips, "Our determined cross-practice," referring of course, to our other new journey about practicing sex again after so many years. Another nice metaphor and I comment the title of our book should be *Metaphors: A Reverse Love Story*. But are these metaphors or just code words for our private use, or both? Need to think about this. Later we warm up as usual by each positioning near the net and hitting soft volleys to each other and this morning we break our prior record of 33 with 68 hits in a row in pursuit of our objective of consistency (second only to being in control of "head") in being key to good or even professional play. We agree that we often hit the ball as hard as the pros but what distinguishes the pros is Consistency with a capital C. I say 68, a new record, or better round it off to 69, and Liz says that reminds her of another cross practice we need to pursue.

As we take a water break on nearby grass, a teenage boy with tennis racquet in hand walks by. We comment that he must be a young stud and wonder if he now is like us at that age when wham-bam thank-you-ma'am was the constant focus of those perpetual hard-on days. Liz thinks yes, but I suggest that perhaps with the internet and wide-spread sexual information teenagers today may be more sophisticated. I say I never even knew about blow jobs at that age, whereas today's teenagers get this and much more raunchy sex information easily by internet, including pictures of people actually doing it, and so much more (oral and anal sex, etc.). I joke that given my preoccupation with sex like other guys I knew, I would have become an expert at web navigation given the incentive to read and see such sexual activity. We laugh and again Liz ponders that this just reinforces her point that the pursuit of conquest and male pleasure dominates over mutuality and pleasuring the woman. I respond that probably is so in most cases, but again there must be a certain percentage of male teenagers who are smarter and use the internet information (including pictures of the vagina and clitoris) to pursue the mutuality journey with their girlfriends. So perhaps our *Reverse Love Story* will not resonate with today's teenagers as much as with our Boomer contemporaries.

This morning I don't feel my usual hip and back pain and the need to fight pain versus pleasure of hitting tennis balls with Liz. Perhaps hormones or this tennis exercise in addition to swimming (both yesterday) is helping my arthritis. We discuss the need to find the balance of exercise and restraint that maximizes my pain free movement.

Talking on the bench in the shade, Liz pulls out her iPod and shows me how this is also a camera, including a video camera. She shows me how to work it, although it is so small with such tiny controls that my big fingers have trouble using it. She is also learning how to use it since her video of me was recorded, but not mine of her. She will ask someone at her camera shop. I wonder if this is a prelude to "the gift," which we have not talked about for some time, and I have backed off, thinking my suggested birthday gift might have been an over-the-line request in the first place. We have talked about the problem of keeping such photos or videos private so no one ever has access to such intimate shots.

July 4, 2001. Liz says her old bras are 36-D, but the new ones are 34-D to prop up the aging twins. I have named Bermuda, and said we need to find a comparable metaphor for her big, beautiful, breathtaking breasts, so it hits me that in addition to "the twins" or "the girls," we can call them "Big D" or simply "D" or D-squared (like D-squared for prolonged play). Or a combination, like D-Pack, to combine two of our code words for her. She says any of the above is OK because no one will know what we are talking about — which of course is the beauty of the metaphors. Liz mentioned getting her bras off the rack at a store and I punned that she needed big bras for her big rack, but don't think she got this lame male pun. Also she mentioned the glow (perspiration) from tennis, and I think of glow as in after-glow from sex (poem 7, pg 32), but it works for both via the cross-training metaphor. Word play.

The proposed *Metaphors* book may never happen, but Liz now seems to think it will, and has sent me her first draft of notes. She says perhaps she can use the writing as therapy in discussing family issues. She will use Elizabeth P. Winthrop as her pseudonym. I will use Steven McMann,

the little prince

All my childhood years have passed since
I first read about the Little Prince
And it's only now I have come to sense
Numbers are matters of inconsequence.
We grow up to run down roads near and far
Never quite satisfied with where we are
Busying ourselves with forms of pretense
Rather than that which makes a difference.
We find a lonely space, the land of fears
Next to that secret place, the land of tears.
The Prince's rose and his sheep in a box
Form the heart of the fox's paradox:
We can find the essential if we try
To see what's invisible to the eye.
The flower we bless with care and duty
Becomes uniquely dressed in true beauty.
Thus the Little Prince sees our common faults
A children's tale to benefit adults.

Chapter 12
PLAN B

*t*his was planned to be the first chapter where Liz describes her childhood and comments on my preceding chapter about my childhood memories, thus beginning the double helix intertwining of our separate backgrounds, experiences and perceptions. Liz started to do so with several promising discussions and a few e-mails, but then time passed and eventually I realized that the task was no longer of interest to her or she had more pressing concerns. Hey, there could be a hundred reasons why she did not follow through, including the obvious one of possible embarrassment if her family found out that she was the author or participant in such explicit sex.

Actually, explicit sex may have been a factor, but I don't think a big one, at least as far as her children are concerned. Liz in my experience has always been open and progressive with her children about sex. Instead of wine, which I don't drink and don't know anything about, I brought Liz a copy of Jon Stewart's *America* as a gift that first evening when she hosted the pre-Palestinian speaker dinner. I cautioned Liz that she might have to keep the book hidden from her children due to the explicit sexual references and the shocking pictures of naked U.S. Supreme Court Justices. Liz looked at the pictures, laughed and said "au contraire, I'm going to share this with them." Indeed, the explicit sexual descriptions in *Metaphors* that embarrass me even as I write them probably are passé to Liz's children and an entire generation exposed to Jon Stewart's *Daily Show* and Stephen Colbert's *Report*, to say nothing about the explicit sex so easily available on the internet. If our pseudonyms were penetrated by Liz's children, they probably would not be surprised to learn that their mother was a sexual human being.

More likely, the reason Liz stopped writing was her dysfunctional family — siblings, father and extended family. If the reason was dysfunctional family concerned about their reputations and for Liz's children, I certainly cannot blame her. Whatever the reason, Liz did not specify one when I asked and I decided not to push her to disclose one. Our developing relationship was more important to me than the book. But Liz has a gift for saying so much by saying so little. Did you notice her brief but striking comment in her three sentence e-mail before her contributions suddenly stopped, "I was journaling pain."

Liz said that this was not the case for me. I interpret these comments to mean that unlike me, her attempt to write about her childhood and her dysfunctional family was just too painful. One example is Liz's troubled relationship with her Harvard grad Dad that has never been addressed much less resolved, and so the hurt continues and is worse when she started to write about it. My issues with my deadbeat Dad were over for the most part when I threw him out of the house and out of my existence. He was no longer a factor in my life. Although there is a deep religious and political divide between me and my family — running from my progressive social liberalism on the left to their religious right Tea Party view of the world — we put aside these divisions when we have family reunions and have a great time joking and laughing through the long reunion weekends. Such is hard to imagine for Liz from what little I know about Liz's family. There is substantial irony in the fact that my family which had grown up in poverty had found a way to be happy; and Liz's family which had grown up privileged in great wealth had not. It's a cliché that is often true: money cannot buy happiness.

I share concerns about possible, even likely, disclosure as the author of *Metaphors: A Reverse Love Story*, but have less to lose. For a start, unlike Liz, I have never married or had children so the risk of disclosure to family members is considerably less. I like children, but have never wanted my own, perhaps for reasons evident in Chapter 5 describing my childhood in Milan, Michigan. Over a lifetime of relationships with several women and a great deal of unprotected sex, I am surprised that to my knowledge I have not impregnated any of them. I suspect that I may have been shooting blanks from the start. Also, women are still held to a different standard of conduct regarding sexual exploration outside of marriage. You need not have read Wilt Chamberlain's infamous *A View From Above* to know that men can and do disclose and even brag about their sexual activity without the negative consequences that would befall a woman.

I am disappointed, however, that Liz did not follow through on *Metaphors* as she is a very perceptive woman and writing her part of the double helix, including the complex and subtle mysteries of the gender gap, would have helped us better understand each other and our developing relationship. So on to Plan B. I will continue with my perceptions of our relationship and in place of Liz's anticipated chapters, will expand my story into something more like a memoir. In doing so I am aware that now the book will be twice as self-centered and self-serving as before.

I do not intend for the memoir to be a balanced autobiography. A balanced autobiography should be an honest self-appraisal of one's life, including the dark side. I do not have the energy or inclination to undertake this difficult task, much less disclose and discuss my shortcomings or any of the stupid and negative things that I have said and done over a lifetime. The memoir part of this book will pick and choose some highlights and illustrative memories, some related to the reverse love story and some not. While not as rich as the double-helix alternative, Plan B provides the opportunity to describe parts of my fortunate life before the dread bird-of-time catches up with me. At my age, with Afib, a bad back and various other physical ailments, I may not get another chance before I die — or worse, morph into Alzheimer's or dementia. Some readers may want to skip the memoir chapters to continue with the reverse love story. Vice versa for others who may find the memoir more interesting. Hopefully most readers will find both a good read.

love match

I met her on the tennis court one day
She looked so striking when she asked to play
A friendly set or two of mixed doubles
Portending the start of most my troubles.
We traded points until the score was tie
"Hit my alley," I joked. "If you dare try."
I was well positioned right near the net
With my partner serving to end the set
When she returned serve so hard and fast
I was sure my playing days were past
As the ball hit hard and square on my chest
My racquet and glasses flew off I'll attest
I yelled, "I've been drilled" before coming to rest
Face down on the court too stunned to protest
My ego bruised more than that black & blue scratch
She looked down at me and said, "Game, set and match."
Later she insisted she heard me clearly
Prompt her to go for my belly, not alley.
"Besides it's all your fault you took that fall
Your eyes were fixed on me and not the ball."
Her spot close to my heart has been on display
Ever since I fell for her that summer day
Her mark is on me and you may recall
It's about the size of a tennis ball.

Chapter 13
LOVE MATCH

*t*he light verse titled "Love Match" (facing page) is a fairly accurate account of how Pam and I met on a public tennis court in Boulder. At the time I was unattached and she had recently broken up with a guy who was a control freak. Within a few weeks and after several dates, I asked Pam to move in with me. "I live alone in a big box with six bedrooms, so there's plenty of room, assuming you can live surrounded by books." I helped her move her meager possessions into my house, and it was soon obvious that we were a good match. Pam and I shared a love of tennis and a sense of humor that drew us close together. I informed Sharon in Boston (more below) that I had met a wonderful woman, and therefore would not be able to see her romantically again. But I truly valued our relationship and wanted to remain friends.

Pam and I had paid our $25 annual dues to be members of the Boulder Tennis Association (BTA). By special arrangement with the City of Boulder, BTA would reserve courts for the tournaments it organized for its 40-50 members. The membership consisted of a diverse group ranging from lawyers to the unemployed, and no one cared about socio-economic status (SES). What mattered at BTA was how good your serve was and how strong your backhand. Pam and I met at one of the tournaments memorialized by *Love Match*. We enjoyed competing in almost all of the tournaments organized by the BTA, and my sports room today, in addition to shelves of sports books, displays many trophies won playing singles and mixed doubles at the 4.5 USTA level. Almost all of our social life revolved around BTA, and that was all we needed.

Bones

Driving a busy street one winter day
She spotted a mangy dog on the stray
Eating dirt and some garbage castaway.
Stop now for that poor pup, I heard her say
In a tone that without doubt did imply
Our relationship rode on my reply.
No creature should suffer such agony
I'll find him a good home, she assured me.
So we stopped to rescue this sad canine
With pedigree straight from Heinz fifty-nine
Black matted hair mixed with some marks of tan
Imagine the sorriest dog you can
Then multiply by a factor of three
And his picture you will begin to see.
While we waited for the call from someone
Seeing ads she assured me she had run
He almost ate us out of house and home
Trying to flesh out all the undergrown
Of the fur ball we called Begga Bones.
Bones vacuumed down food from pancake to egg,
And when he peed he lifted one front leg.
No wonder that Bones would stumble and fall
Since he moved forward on a diagonal.

Floppy ears often folded inside out
Bones chased his tail in circles roundabout.
But in spite of all his faults I was told
This pup was special with a heart of gold.
And it was plain for all to see
Her choice of me proved good analogy.
Then she assured me she'd checked many homes
And only ours was good enough for Bones.

Pam was one of the unemployed. I never could figure out why this smart attractive graduate of the University of Wisconsin was unable to secure a job. The anemic job market along the Front Range was certainly a factor, as was the large number of new arrivals attracted to Colorado's mild climate and majestic mountains. I almost cried when Pam was desperate enough to apply for one of the temporary employee jobs that UPS filled to handle the extra workload during the Christmas holidays. She did not get the UPS driver job, but accepted the offer of driver assistant at minimum wage.

Several years later Pam got her big break when Standard & Poors (S&P) hired her at an entry-level database position. It was onerous work, but Pam was happy to have full time employment and an opportunity to show what she could do. Over the next few years she was promoted to increasingly responsible positions, culminating in one of the coveted sales positions. With the benefits of a good salary and unlimited commissions, Pam became a star within the company, earning an income that far surpassed my assistant professor's salary. After several years, she had banked enough to take early retirement and spend full time with her animals at the ranch. It was a great success story not only for Pam, but also for a big corporation that recognized her talent and gave her comparable opportunities. Kudos to Pam. Kudos to S&P.

I could live happily without animals; Pam could not. After many months resisting the idea, I agreed to a compromise. Pam could bring "a little Spike" home from the animal shelter. I had my handyman, Carl, build a knee-high fence to complete existing fencing around my yard. Imagine my reaction when Pam brought home from the animal rescue shelter a German shepherd mix ("McDuff") big enough to literally step over the knee-high fence. At substantial expense Carl returned to rip out the knee-high fence he had built days earlier, and replace it with a head-high fence. McDuff proved to be a great companion, but Pam worried that he might be lonely. That problem was solved when she rescued a mangy mutt drinking dirty water from a street curb, as detailed in *Bones* (poem 19, pg 134). The mangy stray we named Bones captured our hearts with his goofy ways and unlimited energy. When Bones developed an inoperable brain tumor many years later, Pam expended her limited savings for an MRI in a hopeless attempt to find a cure. I was appalled at the $2,000 expense, and asked Pam how much she would spend to save Bones. Her reply, "Everything." I remember the lump in my throat that day as I realized that Pam was a much better person than I ever would be. Bones died a few days after the MRI confirmed the obvious, inoperable brain cancer. In the days preceding his demise, Bones, seemingly sensing his end, would jump up onto the bed to comfort us. I still miss that goofy mutt. See *Farewell Bones*, (poem 20, pg 137)

Years later the story would repeat itself. I came home from work one day to find an abused horse in my backyard (poem 21, pg 141).

Farewell Bones
1987 – 1995

Farewell good buddy, good old begga Bones
Who helped turn our house into a home.
You limousine-stretched from poor starving stray
Into Pam's prized purebred Huntaway.

You came as a dog, but left as our pal.
How can we forget each game ritual?
Your head under blanket you'd ostrich hide,
While exposing with butt-rolls your backside.

Tossing ball or leash on paper or book,
Making us play attention by hook or crook,
With goofy look, by our side everywhere,
Sitting so flop-eared straight, such wide-eyed stare.

Greeting each walk by throwing leash and rug,
Later trading a cuddle for a hug.
Leaping into our dreams each night in bed,
Prelude to ritual flop, stretch and spread.

With frequent bark, but never a bite,
You kept ghosts, goblins and gloom from our door.
Now you rest in a place far from fright
Where wind and thunder will scare no more.

We'll miss you like a big hole in our lives,
Yet the special joy you brought us survives.
Your gentle lick like one last kiss goodnight
Rekindles a fire that still burns bright.

It was clear that our ultimate goals differed. After Pam purchased Buckenbite from the neighbor living next to a nearby park, Pam boarded the Arabian paint mare at a ranch about fifteen miles away. She spent more and more time with Buckenbite at the ranch, and her head was increasingly in horse heaven. Pam wanted to live on a ranch with animals both inside and outside the house. I did not. Our sex life had become routine and then dwindled to almost non-existent. Pam explained, correctly I think, that we were both passive lovers, and needed the other to take the initiative. Perhaps we could have worked it out, but when Pam's mother, Pat, began to fail, we decided the best solution was to buy a small five acre ranch with the proceeds of Pat's Boulder house. Pam would be able to live her dream of endless animal care by moving into the ranch to care for her ailing mother.

This was a sad time for all. I had enjoyed Pat's eccentricity and crazy sense of humor. Pat would almost die from anticipation when I would take her with me to sales. With a houseful of outstanding antique country furniture collected in the Milwaukee area years earlier, Pat now was thrilled to buy kitsch — the more outrageous the better (poem 16, pg 116). Kitsch delighted Pat's eccentric core; fine country furniture, not so much anymore.

My hope was that Pam and I would continue our twelve-year relationship as the good friends we had always been. We would get together on weekends for dinner and a movie, and then be happy to return to our respective homes afterwards. We were platonic friends, and neither of us wanted that to change. The new arrangement worked until it didn't. We had agreed that we did not want to stop one another from dating. I was starting to enjoy my monastic life, and had less and less inclination to play the dating game. One day Pam told me about her new relationship with a widower (I call him "the cowboy," no disrespect intended) who lived near her new ranch and also loved horses. This would put a stop to our getting together for platonic dinners on weekends, but she wanted me to come to a pre-Christmas dinner to entertain Pat who missed me (and vice versa). At Christmas she had plans to join the cowboy at his brother's house in North Carolina. I asked Sharon, my long term Boston friend, to join me in Colorado for a few days, but only with the understanding that I did not leave Pam in order to start something different with her. It would be the first Christmas that Pam and I had not spent together in twelve years.

The pre-Christmas dinner with Pam and Pat at their new ranch was a big hit. This was an important transition for me (a kind of emancipation from emotional ties if that were possible) and I think for Pam too. As I wrap gifts for Pam and Pat (they both prefer many small gifts to one big or expensive one), I listen to the Linda Eder tape that Jill sent me. The Michigan stoic, the man who never cries, cries during the beautiful "Letting Go" duet.

It would be hard for the pre-Christmas gathering to be better. Pat's antique ornaments adorn a small tree and she has arranged the toy train and other holiday ornaments into a festive display. Pat, as is usually the case, is starved for attention, wants to dominate the conversation, bringing from various rooms sundry antiques to show and use as launching pads for relived memories of long past persons and places. There will be time for more of this later. I join Pam to help her feed Buckenbite before dinner and delight again in how she loves every little step in the feeding and caring process. As usual, I get bored quickly with such animal activity and want to talk about something, anything, to get her head back from horse heaven to me. In the tack room while she is preparing a special blend of oats, brown sugar and other ingredients for horse dessert we have a chance to talk. We note how almost exactly one year ago her mother was so far `falling down stairs out of it' that an expensive nursing home seemed imminent. Pam said the country ranch has been good for her too and repeated her "This is a dream come true" refrain. I told her about how I had driven Jill, a visiting high school classmate, by the ranch about a week earlier and we had seen her with her horses in the corral but decided not to say hello since her head was so clearly in horse heaven. Pam said be sure to say hello if there is a next time.

All of the other animals, including Duffer Dog, Molly and Bearcat having been fed, we are back inside and Pat is at her witty best. She opens my first gift, an armadillo made from dried manure. She delights in the "pooper pet" box label and exclaims, "This gift is crap." A box of poker cards labeled "Stud" she hurries to undo because Pam and I are joking that it includes vulgar beefcake pictures. After struggling for ten minutes to undo the glassine wrapper, only to discover that all the cards, "Including the joker!" only have horse head pictures, she cries, "What a dirty trick!" She is somewhat appeased however by my third gift, a *Playboy* parody titled "Playboar" with risqué pictures and takeoffs on pigs as fantasy objects, including fold out pig of the month in panties.

We laugh like old times over Christmas dinner. Years ago when Pam went back to work at Standard & Poors, we agreed that it did not make sense for her to cook for me, but tonight she has prepared my favorite spaghetti dish. Pam's head is so often focused in horse heaven and on her other priorities that this treat for me is especially welcome.

I leave shortly after dinner, asking Pat if Pat's pooper pet was her number one best gift and the immediate reply, "No, it's my number two gift." We all laugh and as I leave I succeed in placing unseen, a rubber chicken in the flowerpot hanging outside the bay window, knowing it will be such a shocking surprise for them in the morning.

Mystical Pair

What twist of fate joined this woman-horse pair?
Childhood dream and Arabian-Paint mare.
Why this horse untrained with a rep for mean
Throwing all men and a rodeo queen?

She felt a bond, a common destiny,
Brought this horse of her fear and fantasy.
I'll call you my Mystic, not Bite and Buck.
One will become the other with love and luck.

Rescued from neglect, your free spirit
Will freely submit to my bridle and bit.
Yet rebellion burned from deep inside,
Turned training into roller coaster ride.

By day she trained Mystic, so small and plain,
At night rode in dreams behind a flowing mane
The mare that changed when she began to move
With gait so light and swift, so strong and smooth,

Rider tall and proud, head and tail held high:
Look at me! You never knew I could fly!
All horses and riders turned heads and eyes
As Mystic seemed to dance and double in size.

Her fear and fantasy like magic trick
Transformed into this magical Mystic.
Sometimes it's hard to tell true from what seems.
Was this ride for real, or just in their dreams?

Dear Pam,

Thanks again for the perfect presents, favorite spaghetti dinner and witty good company the other night. I don't think I'll ever forget, "What a dirty trick," "Not #1, #2 gift," and "This gift is crap!"

You said you didn't think you were a different woman today, but to me you seem very different from the woman I first met on the Boulder park tennis courts. You didn't have pets then and your life did not revolve around animal care. You may have known in your heart you never changed, but I watched you evolve from a woman not sure of yourself, your career or direction in life, to the present day confident and strong woman who is so sure animal care is her life that she refuses any compromise in relation to them. All this and more made it clear to me our time had come for letting go. It is the mark of a growing difference in values between us and a mark of your strength. I admire your new strength of purpose and wish you well as you find your own way with it.

Enjoy the holidays with your horsy friends and tell that mother of yours to be careful the way she throws her wit around.
Wishing you all the best,
Steve

When I started to write this summary of my relationship with Pam, I casually wrote "Pam and I separated amicably." In my mind that was true, my boring forest view. I had forgotten about all the trees — all the details of the hurt and pain of separating after twelve good years of living together. I remembered some of the details a few days ago when I came across some contemporaneous correspondence with Jill, our class homecoming queen at Milan Public High School and still a good friend. The letters led me on a walk into the trees. I had forgotten the anguish over a few pieces of wood — the custom shelves that Pat, the lady carpenter, had built for Pam's salt and pepper collection.

Shelf Thoughts

In the months preceding closing on her new ranch house, I re-minded Pam that she had a ton of items around the house that could and should be prepacked to get ready for the movers. I told her she should hire some kids at $8 an hour or have the movers pack since our time, she a Standard & Poors Compustat Account Executive and I, an Assistant Professor at the University of Col-orado in Boulder, is worth so much more than the cost of packers. She said she would take care of it, but as the weeks go by and no sign of packing is evident, I become somewhat nervous about the prospect of Pam moving without taking many of her possessions. She admits that she tends to procrastinate, especially now given the additional time demands of helping her mother get ready for the move; also saying it would help if I could find her moving boxes, tape, etc. This I did, but it did not help as very few of Pam's possessions had been packed by moving day, and therefore the movers who had only partially loaded their van with all of Pam's mother's possessions only took a bed, dresser and a few other of Pam's items to the new ranch.

Concerned about not really getting my house back to clean, organize and decorate the way I wanted (one of the benefits of the new arrangement for me), I reminded Pam many times over the next week that it was not fair for her to treat my house as her personal storage area. With good intentions she assured me that she would get Connie and other friends to come help move the rest of her things. And indeed one day Pam and Connie came to the house in Connie's pick-up truck. I was greatly relieved until I saw them in a basement storage room going through one of the many bags and boxes of old letters and bills that Pam had accumulated over the years. Since it would take hours at that rate just to go through a few bags, I suggested that Pam simply take the bags and boxes with her and sort through them later at her leisure. But Pam didn't want to take any excess to the new house, it started to snow and off she went without taking much of anything from the two main floors of the house that I wanted to clean of accumulated dog hair and reorganize.

The weeks passed and no sign of any additional moving activity. Pam is too busy organizing her new house and tending to the needs of her animals. The animal needs grow as she rescues an old mare, Frosty, that needs immediate attention. Clearly there is no time for Pam to pack and move things from my house when job, mother, animals and new house are more important priorities.

One day it rains. Pam has not taken her raincoat from one of the many closets packed full of her clothing and sundry items. Pam comes to the house in her new Ford Explorer truck to pick up her raincoat. I suggest that she throw a few boxes of things in the empty truck to take back to the new house. She says she is in too much of a hurry to do it now and drives off.

This becomes a pattern. Return to the house to pick up an item or two of immediate need (a colander, frying pan or whatever), but not packing her other pots, pans and related kitchen items that fill the kitchen cupboards and pantry. I offer to help her sort through the kitchen and various closets throughout the house in an attempt to facilitate getting my house back. She does not have time and so I start to do so for her. I pack her clothing, shoes, related miscellany from the various upstairs closets, put them in my car and gradually move many of Pam's items to her new ranch house when I go there to help her move furniture and boxes. Pam is not too pleased that some of her clothing may have gotten wrinkled since I did not pack them carefully enough, but this annoyance passes quickly and I am treated to dinner and some good conversation about her animals and new horsy friends.

Over time I resign myself to the need for me to pack Pam's possessions from the areas of the house I want to clean and organize. I continue to pack boxes for her, but of course for each hour of my time that I am doing so without Pam's help I am not in the best of moods. During one of my phone calls to my good friend Sharon in Boston, Sharon tells me this procrastination is not so surprising because it is obvious that Pam is not psychologically prepared to move out and let go yet. There is some denial and holding on to her prior life and me, Sharon says. I have thought about this before and acknowledge there may be some truth to this, but knowing Pam I believe that it is primarily procrastination with a task that is not as pleasant as other tasks like tending to her animals and organizing her new house. Both could be true.

Pam seems to have plenty of time for lunches, movies and parties with her circle of friends. The ranch with all her animals in the house and horses in the yard is a dream come true and she seems to love it. She is helping her new cowboy friend build additional fencing so the horses can roam free on five acres of the property (with resulting manure on the front steps, patio, etc.). Pam confides in me at one point that she has fallen in love with the cowboy and has been swept away and distracted by this new relationship. I think this is good because for a long time now I have thought what Pam needed was some guy who shared her passion for animals (the way that Pam and I at first had shared a passion for tennis). We each need to go our separate ways but it would be easier for me to go mine if she would meet her moving obligations. I tell her all of this including offering some moral support for her need to find a kindred spirit cowboy.

The weeks pass and gradually I am reclaiming parts of my house through the process described above. From time to time Pam asks about taking some items that were jointly purchased or of uncertain ownership. Most of this I don't care about and she can take what she wants. However, there is one thing that I would like her to leave behind – the custom shelves that her mother had built for Pam's salt and pepper shaker collection.

At one point in our relationship Pam took special pleasure in some of her salt and pepper shakers (mostly animals and other cutesy or funny creatures) and started a salt and pepper shaker collection. Over the years the salt and pepper collection grew to over 300 sets as her mother, I and various friends would give shaker sets to Pam for special and even not so special occasions. To hold and display the salt and pepper collection Pam's mother, Pat, built custom wooden shelves to hang between the front door and the kitchen, even as Pam lost interest in the collection.

Pat is approaching eighty years of age and now needs the kind of live-in assistance that was one of the reasons for the move in the first place. Pat and I get along very well. We have similar senses of humor and enjoy insulting each other, seeing who can make the most clever or witty remark about the other's strengths or weaknesses. In addition to this frequent verbal repartee I have condensed some of my insults and compliments into two poems about Pat, *Lady From Wisconsin* (poem 16, pg 116) and *Lady Carpenter* (poem 22, pg 148), which she has framed and inflicts upon others when proudly showing them off to unsuspecting visitors. If I were not so sure that Pam still enjoys and values my company too, I would suspect that she tolerates me simply because I provide such good provocation and entertainment for her mother.

Pat and I also share an interest in antiques. She loves to tell and I love to hear (except when she starts to tell me a story I have heard twenty times before) the stories behind her wonderful collection of antiques. The house is bulging with antique gadgets of one kind or another and Pat can reminisce so wonderfully about their use and acquisition (an apple peeler, a cherry stone device, etc.). Pat's collection of plain antique country furniture, such a contrast to my heavily carved, dark, ornate antique furniture is exquisite. You can't even buy this quality of country furniture in antique stores anymore. Even a little box of antique marbles is rich in stories as well as actual value and there are dozens and dozens of boxes of this kind of antique stuff all over the house. The market value has to be several hundred thousand dollars, but the emotional and other value to Pat is much more. Pat is very generous and frequently tells me she wants me to have items that I admire, but of course I almost always decline (I have accepted a few books and an interesting wax seal, but nothing of much material value).

This digression about Pam's mother may seem remote from moving problems, but it forms the context for my request to Pam that she leave the shelves behind. I would like to have them as a special gift from and memory of Pat. She made them, they are custom made for my wall and they will be perfect for my collection of small books. The shelves have very little market value but what a perfect gift to leave behind for me to remember Pat by. Pam says she is not sure because Pat needs shelf space for her numerous knick-knacks. I ask her to think about it.

The weeks pass and Pam has not packed her salt and pepper collection, which remains so prominently the first thing visitors see when they enter my house. Finally, again in something of a bad mood, I carefully remove and pack all 300 plus salt and pepper shakers into four cardboard boxes; knowing that Pam has now lost interest in the collection and it is unlikely that they will ever be unpacked for display in her new house. From disparate bookshelves and corners around the entire house I find my collection of small books and spend hours arranging them on Pat's custom shelves, delighting in such a fine home to bring all my small books together for the first time. To my eye the shelves look so much better with the books than they did with the salt and pepper shakers. Every time I walk into the house and by this collection, I will be pleasantly reminded of Pat, who among other things takes such pride in being, rare for her time, a lady carpenter. *Lady Carpenter* becomes the title of one of my poems (below) about this delightful, totally eccentric lady who just happens to be Pam's mother.

Lady Carpenter

The lady carpenter with artistic bent
Met Lutheran lawyer, Missouri Synod sent,
At Early Times bar in old Milwaukee.
Soon son and daughter made a family.
For country farm house, five acres and lake.
Even then so unique, make no mistake,

There was nothing she could not draw or make:
Hand-woven rugs, teddy bears, antique fake.
Painted the Angel Gabriel on barn,
Would talk up a storm while spinning a yarn.
Filled house with fine primitive furniture,
Then carved each piece in exquisite miniature.
With heart of gold, this woman tried to please,
Chauffeured old ladies and helped charities.
So many pets some thought her place a zoo:
Monkey, snake, mynah-bird called Magoo,
Piranha, bunch of dogs and batch of cats;
If it needed a home it found one at Pat's.
Moved to Boulder when she was almost old
To see dear daughter and escape the cold.
Perhaps time or place, no one knew how or why,
Maybe change of scene or Rocky Mountain high,
Transformation so complete like magic trick:
Lady carpenter turned lady eccentric.
Worry each moment from first to last,
Forget the present but photo the past.
Recite each line of limerick risqué,
Then revel in the scandal of the day.
Sagittarius trading arrow for wand:
Crabs, toads and goldfish for indoor pond,
Seashell art, five frogs and blowfish with light,
Garage sale kitsch most would hide out of sight.
Collected stuffed animals like a child:
Tiger, bear, anything bizarre or wild.
Come her favorite night of Halloween,
Kids tricked or treated to this fright scene:
Lady without license or sense of right,

Cornering Shep-haired Ford out of the night.
To crown her queen of eccentricity:
Stuffed flamingo and duck dangling from tree,
Tarantula crawling down window wood,
Gave her a rep throughout the neighborhood.
It could have been worse: a change to mean
Like Wisconsin neighbors Dahmer and Gien.
To comprehend this eccentricity queen,
Thirteenth sign of zodiac is foreseen

A few days later Pam comes by with a friend to pick up some boxes I have packed along with pots and pans for a dinner she is about to prepare for some friends. She seems surprised and annoyed that I have packed her salt and pepper shakers and replaced them on the shelves with my small books. The reaction seems out of proportion to the reality. Hours had been saved since I had packed her collection for her, a task she had been avoiding. The symbolism of it all must be painful for her. She says her mother needs the shelves for her knick-knacks. I quietly and rationally repeat my request that she or I simply buy new shelves for Pat and permit these custom shelves to remain behind as a special memento. Surely Pam knows how much this means to me because it is about the only thing I have asked for, but she declines and says she plans to take the shelves today. I am upset and hurt but try not to show it and simply tell Pam that she will need to take my small books from the shelves herself because I have just done so for her salt and pepper shakers. I go for a long bike ride. When I return Pam and the bookshelves are gone and my small books spread across the kitchen island countertop. What remains is a wall that features boltholes and an obvious need for repainting.

It is approximately July when I lose the bookshelves. I don't comment further on the shelves because I still value all the wonderful things about Pam and don't want to lose her friendship over a few pieces of wood. If I really want shelves for my small books, I can, and later do hire Carl to make them for me.

Small Books and Custom Shelving

The pre-Christmas dinner was a big hit, as described above. It had been the perfect pre-Christmas gathering; and I almost forget earlier seeing the shelves on the tack room floor leaning empty against an unused wall.

I drive back to my city house wondering if the special shelves are my unstated punishment for declining to live at the ranch house with Pam, her mother and all their animal friends. Or is Pam's head so much in horse heaven that she is oblivious to the symbolism of the shelves? As I close my garage door, I also wonder whether it matters.

Jill

Jill had also been a star at our small public high school in Milan, Michigan; homecoming queen, class officer, cheerleader and like me, one of ten distinguished honor students at graduation. At this late stage in our lives we are both unattached. Ollie Prindle and Jean think we would make a good marriage match. I had wondered about some kind of long-term relationship with Jill, but did not want to start another long distance relationship. One with Sharon was enough.

We exchanged a series of letters and phone calls over several months after Pam moved to her ranch. I promised Jill a trip into the mountains if she came to visit me. She did and when we stopped in a Georgetown bookstore on our trip into the mountains, I found a copy of *84 Charing Cross Road*, Helene Hanff's true story of a transatlantic business correspondence for twenty years about used books that developed into a close friendship. I was delighted to hear that it is one of Jill's favorites too. We adopt the conceit that she is Helen and I Frank in the long-distance almost-love story. Watching TV news that evening on my sofa, I made a move on Jill. She pushed me away saying she was not ready for an intimate relationship. I was horrified as I think one of the worst things a man can do is force himself upon an unwilling woman; and one who is a guest in my house makes the faux pas even more offensive. I apologize and am so ashamed I cannot get to sleep that night. I go downstairs and write this poem of apology.

Prayer to Jill

Please forgive him his trespass
Turned splendor into gender mess
Confusing one of your No's
As a maybe or even Yes.

A cliché since time began
The mind's the measure of the man
But whether peasant or king
Men too often think with their thing.

Since he did not intend to offend
Let him remain your special friend.

I give her the poem in the morning and she dismisses it as unnecessary. "It's not a big deal, Steve, women deal with unwanted advances all the time. You at least backed off immediately."

I tell her that at our age it is unlikely we will find `the one true love.'

She is adamant, "No way. I will find him."

After Jill leaves for Lansing I find and mail her my mother's copy of the Milan Public High School yearbook. Earlier when Jill and I paged through my yearbook to identify and update each other on classmates, she says she regrets her copy was lost in one of her many moves. I know that Jill will not mind the fact that my mother has signed her name in ink on the flyleaf.

Dear Jill,

I am so pleased that you will treasure my mother's copy of our high school yearbook.

I am intrigued by your comments on "Moving On: Shelf Thoughts," which I again apologize for inflicting upon you. You ask why I am so tolerant. Apart from the fact that my version is self-serving and Pam probably could write a counterpart that shows her beyond the call of duty tolerance of an eccentric bibliomaniac, consider this – I don't like conflict. Saw too much of it as a kid in Milan. Conflict turns me off. Why did I become a lawyer then, I hear you ask. It was the combination of making a good living (turning nothing into many things) and the attraction of great constitutional issues (church and state, state and federal, individual and society, etc.) without much consideration for the fact that both involve substantial conflict resolution. I get enough conflict at work, and don't want to bring more into my private life. Pam and I never functioned at an open conflict level. Some would say this would be better and I know some couples thrive on open conflict. Pam might deal with conflict better than I but I doubt it. We are alike in many ways.

I have such a low tolerance for conflict that I would probably resent and retreat at the first sign of open anger or hostility; so I tolerate for my own benefit. In addition, to continue the rationalization, my observation is that the value of open conflict is overrated and usually is counterproductive in both personal and professional life. In both areas I can accomplish my goals better through tolerance than conflict. My goal with Pam is to preserve the best part of our twelve-year relation-ship (our friendship) and don't you think that is more important than a few pieces of wood? I put my frustrations on paper, shared them with a thereby unfortunate intimate stranger and now am moving on to better things.

So regarding your question about emotional conflict versus march-ing to a different drummer, I've always seen myself marching from Michigan to Massachusetts to Colorado to a different drummer. In fact I delight in such marching and pull an important part of my identity from it. The conflict avoidance and/or different drummer life choices may not work for everyone, but I think them best for me. How do you deal with conflict and relationships? How do you answer the conflict and drummer questions you put to me?

Letting go. Yesterday morning I was listening once again to Linda Eder's deeply moving "Letting Go" song, thinking about how much Pam had given me over the years. I so delighted in the child in her which, unlike me, she is unafraid to show and live. Preopening Christ-mas presents, wanting many of them instead of just one, dreaming about being a wild stallion running free along the tide as we walk a Maryland beach, spurring on an imaginary horse from an imaginary saddle straddling the arm of my sofa, etc. All this stimulated me to write light verse poetry to try to capture so as not to lose this wonder-ful experience; and she so appreciating it all. She would read my light verse and tears of appreciation would reward the writing of it. Some she would even frame and hang on the wall and thus convince me to keep writing since one person's genuine appreciation is enough to make it worthwhile. With such rewards you don't need a wider audience, publication, prizes or other affirmation that your writing is any good. "Letting Go" was still playing in the background. I sat down to write a poem titled "Letting Go."

Letting Go

With friendship so fine yet
Let's sing our Letting Go duet
This eve of first Christmas apart
Since our first love match start
Over twelve years ago
I've watched the real woman grow.

You've grown so quietly strong
Now you can sing Letting Go song.
The woman I now know
Didn't exist twelve years ago
Which is why now I know
Your time has come for letting go.

From his house of books this city boy
Looks to country girl living her true joy.
Your pets in house and horses in yard
So thought letting go easy, but it's still hard.
Which is why I now know
My time has come for letting go.

You have given me so much
Sparked my poor poetic touch
Yet we've grown so far apart
Since our first love match start
Over twelve years ago
Which is why we both know
Our time has come for letting go.

You're already finding your way
And you know now I must find mine.
So far apart, yet friends to stay,
We'll be each other's lifeline.
So with friendship so fine yet
Let's sing our Letting Go duet.

You, Jill, were such a refreshing change. You were so focused on me over the weekend. I felt self-conscious about it at times, but I loved it! You, my intimate stranger, listened to my ramblings, you made me coffee in the morning, you helped put away the dishes, you suggested a pattern for reupholstering my kitchen chairs and how to improve my window-well library, etc.

Anyway I know there are tradeoffs with everyone. Martha Stewart might drive me crazy at the other extreme. Pam was very special in what she gave me. I tried to put this into my *Letting Go* poem but Linda Eder's song expressed the feeling so much better that I recorded it to go along with the poem. In fact, the song is so powerful that I fear it expresses more than I feel. Pam didn't have time to play the tape but as expected there were tears of appreciation when she read the poem that more than compensated for my efforts.

I notice on the kitchen counter a recipe for some wonderful treat. I see it and think Pam is about to bake something special for us before I realize that the brown sugar, oats and similar ingredients are for a horse treat that she is planning to cook up for Buckenbite. I tell Pam about my misinterpretation. She thinks it is cute and we both laugh but, like the inevitable dog hair sticking to my suit derriere when she and her dogs lived with me, there is some hurt and disappointment in my laugh.

The next time you are here. Will there be a next time? I understand your decision to stay in Lansing and teach special classes part time for borderline eighth graders. Teaching is God's work and She approves. You know how I know this? I of all people know what tremendous impact a good teacher or two can have on a child's life and this kind of impact on even one child can make it all worthwhile. The chance to design your own curriculum and still permit free time for other things is well worth the trade off in dollars if you can make do.

Let me know your thoughts as time goes by. Please remember that it is not just Frank sending letters across vast distances in *84 Charing Cross Road*. Is there another analogy here? Should the intimate stranger at the other end of Frank's letters have forgotten about her teeth and flew off to be with Frank for a time before it was too late?

I leave you on a lighter note with a gender quote:
Why are women wearing perfumes that smell like flowers?
Men don't like flowers. I've been wearing a great scent.
It's called new car interior.
—Rita Rudner (b.1956)

With loving feelings, I remain your emerging Charing Cross Correspondent.

Steve

Sharon

Breaking up is so hard to do. Letting go is never easy. Eventually one gets over it. The trees, the all-important details, start to fade as time enables one to see the forest more than the trees. I will provide another example as it helps complete the picture, but again this is my self-serving view, and the woman on the other side may have, probably does given the gender gap, a very different account.

Before I met Pam I had a long-term relationship with Sharon. We had met when I was at Harvard Law School and she was working at the Massachusetts State Department of Education (MSDE) near Boston. The details involved in our relationship will have to be left for another time, but suffice it to say that we enjoyed each other's company so much that we would occasionally see each other when our schedules permitted her to fly out to Colorado, or me back to Boston. In other words, not much, but spread out over many years.

One of the reasons I was so attracted to Sharon was her unique combination of feminine and feminist. In her publications and presentations Sharon projected her true self – a strong voice for the betterment of both boys and girls in public education, and for the Mark Shields' kind of Democrat and David Brooks' kind of Republican who can sometimes find common ground beyond partisan gridlock. I like to think that the same is true of me in pursuing the civic standard in public education. In other words, a hard sell in our divisive times. In more personal terms, Sharon and I shared a preference for "character" books and movies over the "crash and burn" alternatives, small gatherings over large parties, private discussions over public meetings, etc.

To outsiders, Sharon and I probably appeared a good match. But most of our years "together" were in a long-distance relationship – she in Boston and I in Boulder. We never had a chance to live together on a daily basis and to experience what that would have been like. During those infrequent times when we managed to get together, it was always as if we were on a honeymoon. Even when we both lived in Cambridge we rarely were together by ourselves for long.

Our relationship was complicated by the fact that Sharon is the divorced mother of a special needs child. Tami was born with cognitive and physical problems; the latter requiring periodic surgeries over the years that never quite managed to remedy the old problems or the new ones that developed. As a result Sharon was faced with endless problems. Terri's erratic behavior, finding a school or work alternative, transport to and from every activity, a sitter for times when Sharon's job prevented direct supervision, arranging appointments for specialist doctors and surgeons, for operations, for recovery and fighting the various bureaucrats and laws inadequate to help finance it all. And Tami's calls in the middle of the night for various things, including changing and washing soiled sheets.

And it never stops. Tami will not graduate into an independent future. The best that can be hoped for is a separate nearby condo with a live-in helper, usually a transient student needing room, board and a small stipend. It seems to me more than overwhelming, and I ask Sharon how she manages it all. Sharon, a Wellesley graduate with a PhD from the University of Minnesota, says, "Yes, I get tired, very tired, but what choice do I have? I am fortunate to have an interesting job, decent pay and influential friends. Think of what it must be like for parents who have none of these advantages." Like my mother, Sharon had more than her share of burdens, and yet managed to survive and even prosper. In spite of the above, Sharon was delightful company and a pleasure to be with both in and out of bed.

Tami saw me as a threat to her mother's attention, and I resented the bad behavior that resulted. A mother's love knows no bounds, and Sharon was a saint in her endless struggles to provide the best life possible for her daughter. I saw what I think Sharon could not see, a manipulative side of Tami. Despite her cognitive and physical problems, Tami was a beautiful child with bright blue eyes and golden hair like her mother. She could be totally charming at times but not so much at others. One day I'll never forget is when we went to Tami's special education school to celebrate the end of another school year. Tami was in the middle of one of her tantrums, probably because I was there and receiving too much of her mother's attention. Suddenly Tami stopped yelling, and did a 180-degree turn from brat to charming. I looked around and saw the reason. One of Tami's teachers had entered our little circle. Tami clearly could control her behavior when she wanted. Perhaps not all the time, but certainly this time. Sharon and I both knew that living together was never a possibility because I, like her ex-husband before, could not deal with Tami's endless problems. Sharon had no choice.

Tami could not keep up with her peers either cognitively or physically, but perhaps to compensate, her emotional intelligence is off the charts. She surpasses almost everyone in her ability to read and manipulate others in order to make her limited harsh world work for her. Perhaps like a blind person who adapts to be more sensitive to sound, Tami's cognitive limitations lead to greater emotional intelligence. Everyone, except for me who Tami clearly sees as a threat to her special relationship with her mother, just loves Tami.

Sharon tried to make it work, with Tami, me and the demands of a full time job at MSDE. One time before, I had left Sharon for the close comfort of Pam. This time seemed harder. Perhaps because Sharon saw some light at the end of the tunnel with Tami settled into her own nearby condominium with the help of a full time assistant, and her well-deserved retirement only a few years away. Then I met Liz, and pulled the plug on Sharon for the second time. When I knew that a long term relationship with Liz was possible, I sent Sharon an e-mail saying I had met a woman I really liked, was lonely, needed some close comfort and therefore would not be able to see her romantically again. But I hoped we could remain friends because I truly valued her friendship. As you can imagine, this did not go over well and it was years before Sharon and I were on speaking terms again. Is there any good way to break up?

Within a year of our separation, Pam met a guy who could give her what I could not: a ring. The cowboy was a widower who lived nearby and shared Pam's love for horses and other animals. When Pam told me that he volunteered two days a week at an assisted living home, I realized that both were better persons than I. I met the cowboy one time when he drove his Ford 150 truck to pick up the two unused doghouses from my back yard. I helped him move the heavy doghouses around the house and into the truck bed. He seemed like a nice guy. I hoped we could all be friends, and even get together for drinks or dinner with Liz sometimes because Liz said she would have no problems with that, but the cowboy could not deal with such complication. He sees me as a threat and has an uneasy agreement with Pam that she can see me occasionally for lunch, but he doesn't want to know anything about it and we are not to communicate otherwise. As a result Pam and I only get together for platonic lunches on our birthdays and at Christmas. It's better than nothing.

So here's the key question for the wheat/chaff discussion. Is this Chapter thirteen wheat or chaff? The chapter takes the reader and me on a digression into my past with Pam, Jill and Sharon. I went there to illustrate how my mind had shut out all of this detail as chaff to see if there was some wheat left over that was worth salvaging. But has all this digging up the past been worth it?

The editor in me says Chapter thirteen is a lengthy digression, which is not necessary to the central *Reverse Love Story* (RLS). The editor of *Metaphors* may well say Chapter thirteen should be jettisoned as the book is morphing too long already. The RLS could proceed without Chapter thirteen, so in this sense it is chaff even though it does reveal a lot about Steve's mind and history. The small bookshelves, for example, are a metaphor for how an entire relationship can get summarized and then simply forgotten as we move on with our lives. In other words, Chapter thirteen is chaff for the central RLS, but wheat for the *Memoirs* part of the book. Readers can judge for themselves, and perhaps some already have by skipping Chapter thirteen and moving on — like a built-in reader-editor.

My conclusion is that what is chaff and what wheat, like "what is value" and many other key issues in life, is a variable concept. Chapter thirteen may be chaff to some readers who want the RLS to move fast forward. But Chapter thirteen is wheat for those who want to slow down and examine Steve in more detail. There is no right answer. Take your pick, or even some mix of each. The chaff-wheat distinction is not absolute, but depends largely upon your purpose.

working mother

She with seven children to raise and feed
Worked her whole life with no care for own need.
Divorced a drunk when she was forty-three
To protect what was left of her family.
Medical Records, her job title read,
Paid just enough to keep kids clothed and fed.

Saw oldest to college, then retail stores,
Troubled kids one counseled, after farm chores.
Another earned an attorney's degree,
Courtesy of Harvard-Rhodes legacy.
Church music the two daughters played and sung.
To frozen North Woods the carpenter son.

Preacher in distant lands the youngest boy:
God's work filled his mother with as much joy
As sixteen grandchildren to multiply,
Assuring her memory will never die.
Moving from small town to big city delight
With a new church to visit every night.

Then only days before she could retire,
A cancer cut short her deferred desire.
And in a new world of sex equity,
The long-divorced drunk ironically
Collected all her social security.
Perhaps he too deserved some charity.

Oh working Mother, your work is now done.
You should have been given more time for fun.
We owe a debt we can never repay.
Your love for us spoke more than we can say.
Mother who toiled to give us everything,
Rest in peace where the choirs always sing.

Chapter 14
WORKING MOTHER

his book is dedicated to my mother. The frontispiece features her childhood picture circa 1919. It is the only thing I wanted from her meager estate, and I thank my siblings for obliging. The eldest daughter of a second generation of German immigrants who toiled on nearby Michigan farms, my mother had a hard life. Somehow on a medical record librarian's salary, she managed to raise her five children. All graduated from college, and today are respectable, law-abiding citizens.

Although sharing the fundamentalist religious beliefs commonplace in the community in which we lived, she firmly believed in public education. We all benefited from her example of showing teachers the respect they deserve in a relatively low-paying and low-status profession; that they nevertheless find worthwhile for the sake of the children they teach.

Learning
When just a youngster my mother advised
That my teachers at school epitomized
All that was true and good as well as wise
And they in fact proved very good to me
Expanded knowledge and opportunity.

Today it should come as no surprise
When teachers we degrade and criticize
Students now learn less I hypothesize
Since they to us like we to them you see
Both ways are self-fulfilling prophecies.

Seeking a better life for her children and herself, after she completed some business courses at a nearby community college, my mother moved her children from the family farm to a small town about twenty miles away. Perhaps she would have found it easier to stay on the farm, but probably not her children.

My mother lived for her children and her fundamentalist religion — her only social life given the realities of our situation. The two came apart in my youthful rebellion. I used to joke that I was the black sheep in our family even though a Harvard graduate.

Not true. She never stopped believing in my redemption, and was quietly proud of my achievements. I think that over the years she confided in me more than anyone else, and we always enjoyed our infrequent reunions.

She and her children benefited from small town life, but my mother resented the lack of privacy common to small towns. Everyone knew everyone and their business. I don't know what secrets she had to conceal. I like to think that I was the result of some secret romantic rendezvous that gave her temporary escape, but I doubt it. In any case, sometime after I graduated from college she moved from small town to big city. In Lansing she could go to a different church every night of the week, and no one would know or care. At the time I thought the move was a mistake, but I helped her buy a house with the proceeds of her old house, and she seemed happier in Lansing than before.

Surviving on a low-paying job she had found in a state welfare office in Lansing, my mother looked forward to the day she could retire on the social security she had contributed to all her working life. When eligible for social security at age 62, she retired from a life of work. Full time to explore and enjoy more churches! Within a year she was diagnosed with colon cancer, and died after several months of painful (and what I then and still believe were unnecessary) chemotherapy treatments.

It would be comforting to believe that my mother is now enjoying the rewards of the heaven in which she believed, but of course I cannot. To this day I am disgusted with a second irony aggravating the first: the social security payments which she received for only a few months were transferred to her deadbeat divorced husband who had contributed zero to the fund. In an enlightened attempt to protect the many divorced housewives unjustly denied social security payments when their exes died, feminist advocates some years earlier had been successful in pushing through a legislative remedy. The remedy mandated gender equality.

isaac newton

In sixteen sixty-six at twenty-three
Newton left Cambridge University
When a plague caused Isaac's isolation,
He conceived universal gravitation:
Force declining by distance inverse square
On earth, the moon or stars or anywhere.
The Principia records his notion
Of the four laws governing all motion.
Then he, without intent to puzzle us.
Invented differential calculus.
Isaac Newton's insight even proved right
When reflecting on the nature of light.
Newton found a world full of myths and flaws
He left a system of unified laws.
Then Einstein examined Newton's notion
Proved there's no absolute time or motion.
By his theory of relativity
Our world is not what it appears to be.

darwin

Around the world in HMS Beagle
From shell to gazelle, beetle to seagull
Darwin collected every specimen
Then he studied them again and again
Until chancing upon the solution
That proved his theory of evolution.
Inspection of his fossil collection
Suggested that natural selection
Based upon survival of the fittest
Passed the test that ended his lifelong quest.
Then Darwin proved in The Descent of Man
A grand experiment since time began.
Though humans come in varied shades and shapes,
It's evident all share descent from apes.
Thus began the dispute still debated
Whether we evolved or were created.

Chapter 15
HARVARD

Poor Boy at Harvard

My first impression of Harvard was favorable. My roommates were not the academic nerds that I feared, but interesting, diverse, articulate and bright. If I did not have basketball and my studies to fill my time, I could have spent most of my time socializing and thereby getting a good education.

More important to me in those early days at Harvard was the physical comforts that were provided as a matter of course. For the first time in my life I was given three meals a day. The Harvard Union served us meals cafeteria style, and one could eat as much as wanted. I had never eaten so well — meat, vegetables, salad, dessert, available at every meal and I rarely missed a meal. I never disclosed how shocked I was to hear classmates' complaining about how awful the food was, and making plans to go to Harvard Square restaurants where a good meal could be purchased. The nor'easters that occasionally blew through Cambridge could make it as bitter cold as the Michigan winters I was used too, but the dorms were well heated, and I enjoyed the luxury of sleeping in heated rooms for the first time. Unlike most of my classmates, I was grateful for the food and shelter and other physical comforts that Harvard provided as a matter of course.

The financial aid package provided by Harvard was generous for me because it was based on need. Given my impoverished circumstances, my need was great and my consequent full ride scholarship was generous, but all recipients were expected to supplement their stipends with summer and term-time earnings.

My first term-time job involved walking each morning from my dorm in the Yard to Harkness Commons at the North end of Harvard Law School (HLS), where I would take dirty dishes to be washed from the breakfast trays passed by HLS students through an opening in the wall. I could see about half of their headless bodies through the opening, never dreaming that one day I would be an HLS student on the other side of the wall.

My first year at Harvard was very difficult academically. A big shock came at the end of the first grading period in the fall when I had 3 D+'s and 1 C-. I was even more shocked when someone said that freshman grades were sent back to your parents and your secondary school as a matter of course. My poor grades earned me a summons to the Dean's office, where Fred Jewitt questioned whether I was putting too much of my time into basketball. I told him the solution was not so easy as I had been putting in long hours with the books, but in any case if I could not play basketball, which was my love and basis of self-esteem, I would leave Harvard. He replied that would not be necessary, and I should continue with basketball, but perhaps I should focus on studying more effectively rather than longer and harder. I soon learned that academic success at Harvard was not necessarily mastering content, but appearing to do so.

I was spending hours reading each page of every book on each course's reading list, and was one of the few naïve enough to do so. The trick was to focus less on the trees, and more on the forest; to have perspective on the bigger picture, rather than become overwhelmed by the details. To put it another way, the trick was to game the system, and learn how to bullshit on an exam as did the successful students. I learned enough about how to play this Harvard academic game to improve my first year grades to respectable B's.

As I read the prior paragraph, I realize that it is only partly true. More important I think was the critical analysis I learned in Humanities 6, a notoriously difficult course that I had taken only because it fit my schedule. Hum 6 as it was called was a lifesaver. Taught by Professor Reuben Brower, and his section men and women, the course emphasized close and analytical reading of text, focusing on every word in context, and researching word derivations. In other words, at the opposite extreme of seeing the forest instead of trees, this course examined each branch and leaf of a single tree, analyzing each word in great detail. Other English courses would encourage you to read biographies of the author and period history to gain greater understanding of the text. Brower's approach discouraged such outside perspective in favor of the text itself and drawing logical conclusions based thereon. The outside reference encouraged was not biographies or histories, but the Merriam Webster's Dictionary (MWD) or Oxford English Dictionary (OED) to research word derivations. Hum 6 gave me the intellectual and logical tools that would prove invaluable for all of my courses, and my grades improved dramatically, so at the end of the first year I had respectable B's. Applying the same analytical tools learned in Hum 6, my B's turned increasingly into A's, and in my senior year I was named to Harvard's Phi Beta Kappa Society. My roommates who had watched me struggle my freshman year were astounded.

But I'm getting ahead of myself here. Back to freshman year in the Yard.

Don Ransom

In Hollis Hall, my freshman dorm in the Yard, very few of my classmates fit my stereotype of the Harvard nerd. I was pleased to be paired with Don Ransom as my roommate. Don, an army brat who had the sophistication acquired from growing up on bases around the world…but as I start to describe Don, I remember that I have a copy of a December 1997 letter I sent him which says it better. Don had just responded to my holiday letter mentioning that Pam had moved to a ranch to care for her ailing mother and Buckenbite. He remembered my frustration with Andrea, my high school sweetheart, who always seemed more focused on her horse than me.

12/26/97

Dear Don,

I was touched by your recall of "The Woman & the Horse" conversations we had so many years ago at Harvard College. You are one of the few then who will appreciate the "full-circle irony" involved in enclosed holiday letter to friends.

Your perceptive comment reminds me of the special place you hold in my memory and how sad it is that friendships like these tend to get lost in the different directions we take over the years. I am always struck by how carefully most of my women friends carefully cultivate and continually connect with their friends throughout various life cycles, and how most of my male friends and I do not; under the assumption of continued friendship. When/if we get together again there is much we could laugh and talk about.

Last week a friend who I had lost touch with since high school treated me to a long weekend of laughs and shared high school memories. She had as many anecdotes about foolish as well as the good things said and done back then as I. It was not only fun, it was, for me, therapeutic. When/if I will share a few similar things with you about our college days, including some that embarrass me even today when something reminds me of them. One of them involves Bob Abrams. One evening at dinner in Kirkland House I, without thinking, said something like, "You could always Jew him down." It was an expression often used back in my Michigan hometown, which no Jews or other minorities called home. I looked up and saw the hurt in Bob's eyes. I said, "Sorry, Bob, I wasn't thinking." If I ever see Bob again I wonder if I would make things worse by apologizing again. Sometimes it only takes a few seconds to destroy a friendship.

In talking about high school classmates, one of the intriguing things was how our own perceptions of our self can differ so greatly from those of our classmates. It seems intriguing and important to understand these differences and have a sense of which is closer to reality. I had these thoughts in mind when we saw "Amistad" and that night drafted my version of the movie and the hero myth. With your background in psychology, I am sure you would have some interesting insights on these issues. Don't miss the movie, in any case, since it is inspiring to see how well our legal system, including its lawyers, can work.

I wonder if you know what a positive influence you were for me during our college days? As you know, I focused on basketball and my studies, and never shared my thoughts and feelings much. You were my first contact with the big world outside of Milan, Michigan. I always admired you as the golden boy who had everything — handsome, smart, athletic, likeable and socially graceful. Was this your perception of yourself? Anyway, I learned a great deal from you. This may sound mundane, but when I put my business tie on the morning after receiving your welcome letter I suddenly recalled that I was using the same tie technique that you taught me back in 1961 when coat and tie were required for meals at the Union. Until you took the time to show me how to tie a tie, I was leaving my one perfect tie tied as I *pulled it over my head for the next use. Not all that I learned was so mundane. It would be great to see you again. Let's get the gang together again at the next reunion.*

Best,

Steve

Don proved to be a good friend as well as fortuitous roommate. His social skills aided my transition into the social life in Hollis Hall and later as an upper classman at Kirkland House. Don and I overlapped briefly on the freshman basketball team. He confided in me later that he regretted his decision to drop basketball in favor of the rigors of crew under the demanding legendary coach, Harry Parker. I could understand that. Crew in my view was for masochists. Getting up at 5 a.m. on cold winter mornings to excruciating practice in the boathouse tank. I saw how hard and long they practiced first in the tank and later on the Charles River. Compared to the harsh demands of crew under Parker, hoopsters had it easy. Two hours chasing a round ball on hardwood in a heated gym under a laid back coach, Floyd Wilson, who understood that sports at Harvard took a back seat to academics and social life, was much easier. Don said it wasn't the hard work, but the camaraderie of playing basketball with Merle, Barry, Keith and the rest of the team and knowing he could have made a valuable contribution. Don didn't have to explain any further; I knew exactly what he meant.

Bill Drayton

Ironically, the first classmate to fit my unfortunate stereotype of the Harvard nerd was William Drayton II — who became one of my best friends from that freshman class of 1965 through all the years to today in 2014 (53 years!), with at least a few more to come. Bill, a mild mannered, soft-spoken intellectual New Yorker who had prepped at Exeter, looked like Gandhi in coat and tie, a slight fellow whom a strong wind might blow away. I, on the other hand, probably appeared what I was, a six foot six basketball jock weighing in at a muscular two-ten. Bill and I met by chance after a lecture in Nat Sci 10 — "Rocks for Jocks" — a gut course for jocks and others with little interest in science who needed an easy science course to fulfill one of Harvard's general education requirements. I knew what I was doing there, but what about Bill? One day he confided in me that science was never his strong point. Ironically, for several years now Bill sends spectacular photos from remote mountain settings into which he has backpacked. Even after spinal fusion surgery, I can walk only about a block before the pain and fatigue in my back forces me to sit down and rest.

After that fortuitous meeting after a Nat Sci 10 lecture, Bill would often invite me and others to an Indian restaurant somewhere in Harvard Square to discuss his ideas for changing the world. He had this idea that for small change we could change the world, or at least make it better for some poor souls in India where $500 could change multiple lives if invested in the salary of an innovative Indian schoolteacher with an alternative to typical Indian rigid rote-memory schooling.

Later this idea was translated into reality when Bill founded Ashoka: Innovators for the Public, and funded Gloria de Sousa as its first Ashoka fellow. The idea behind Ashoka was simple, even if its' implementation was not. Like a venture-capital firm, Ashoka seeks high yields from modest, well-targeted investments. It seeks returns not in profits but in advances in all social change fields. Today over 3,000 Ashoka fellows worldwide are changing the world with their innovative ideas for social change and social entrepreneurship as defined and practiced by Bill's Ashoka. Ashoka has become recognized and implemented worldwide with the financial support of a loyal group of contributors, including progressive individuals (influential professionals like professors, doctors, lawyers and such) as well as major foundations.

Many argue, as does Michael Edwards in *Small Change: Why Business Will Not Change the World,* that such business models and social entrepreneurship are doomed to yielding small change rather than big dollar lasting impact. From my professor's podium at the University of Colorado in Boulder, I tell my students that the historical record supports Edwards' claim, but that Bill's Ashoka is a dramatic exception to the rule. I attribute this to a combination of Bill's unique intellect, pragmatism, empathy and determination to make a difference, and I wonder if Ashoka can survive when Bill is no longer there to lead.

But Bill will leave for history to decide if or to what extent Ashoka has made a substantial impact. What is indisputably clear today is that Bill, the quintessential example of the social entrepreneurs Ashoka seeks to identify and fund, is recognized as the architect of social entrepreneurship. For his groundbreaking work with Ashoka, Bill has earned honors that would take pages just to list — but one says it all: the genius grant from the MacArthur Foundation.

I am honored to call Bill my friend and proud to have played a very modest role in writing several articles and participating in other fund-raising activities for Bill and Ashoka over the years. For more about Bill and Ashoka, see David Bornstein's *How to Change the World: Social Entrepreneurs and the Power of New Ideas.*

In later years Bill and I agreed that Nat Sci 10 turned out to be an excellent course. We took field trips to examine first hand geological formations along New England road cuts. We learned about carbon dating as the key to understanding geological time and confirming Darwin's theories of evolution. We learned about the scientific method — the method of research in which a hypothesis, formulated after systematic collection of data, is tested empirically. Just as important to me, I got my first "A" at Harvard in Nat Sci 10, giving me much needed confidence that I could do well academically at Harvard.

Social Life

Hum 6, "the trees not the forest course" discussed at the outset of this chapter and Chapter 4, also changed my cultural perspective. Almost fifty years later I still remember my Hum 6 section man reading aloud a paragraph from James Joyce's *Portrait of the Artist as a Young Man* (Ulysses?). The paragraph, which the section man praised as beautifully conceived and written, shocked me since the focus was on the protagonist reflecting upon his life while observing his penis floating in his bathwater.

Sex, which preoccupied my high school classmates and me and was rarely discussed openly or graphically, was the norm at Harvard. One sunny spring day after an impossibly cold and long winter, I joined some classmates to bask in the sun on the banks of the Charles River. The topic soon turned to women, how hard it was to meet them and then wish lists for what we would wish for in a woman. One of the more worldly and sophisticated guys stated, "I want to make sure that the woman I marry is not a virgin."

"You mean someone who is a virgin," I corrected.

"No, fuck no," he replied, "A virgin is to be avoided at all cost."

"You must be kidding, why would you not want a virgin?"

"Why would you want to marry a virgin? Think about it."

I thought about it and concluded that he was right. The first time inevitably is a disaster. Too fast, too fumbling, too disappointing. Better to be with a woman who had been through that and would have more realistic expectations; and know how to make it better. In other words, an experienced woman.

The theory was good, but in fact it was hard to get together with any woman at Harvard. Our freshman class consisted of 1200 males and no females. Harvard's sister school, Radcliffe, which shared classes with Harvard, admitted only about 200 in each class. The ratio was not favorable, especially for me as a recognizable jock. Whereas being a star athlete in high school was a chick magnet, I soon learned to disguise the fact around Cliffe's, as they were called and at nearby women's colleges like Wellesley, because jocks were usually dismissed as unintelligent and undesirable. Unlike high school where half the class would be female and you got to know them casually, the Harvard experience made it difficult for transplants like me to meet women outside of awkward formal mixers and dating situations. The result was that many of my classmates and I rarely dated. New England students could capitalize on their secondary school contacts. For many of us outsiders, our social lives were restricted; in other words miserable.

I finally caught a break (a good one) in the dating department.

James, "I need to find a date for my girlfriend's friend. She's a real looker. Are you interested?"

Steve, "You're putting me on, aren't you?"

James, "No, for real. My girlfriend, Kate, is coming from Greenwich to see me this weekend, but her parents insist on a chaperone. Her name is Linda, and I'd give her a 7 ½ on a 10-point scale. We can't abandon her, so I'm going to fix Linda up with you. It's your lucky day."

Steve, "Count me in. *My Fair Lady* just opened in Boston and I'd really like to see it. Perhaps the four of us could go together?"

James, "Are you kidding? The whole point is to get Linda out of the way so Kate and I can have some private time."

Later on the big night James and I met Kate and Linda for a drink in a bar near Harvard Square. First impression — Linda is drop-dead gorgeous, but perhaps a bit superficial. Not a problem on my part as I am more horny than particular. After a socially acceptable time together, Linda and I waved goodbye to James and Kate as we headed for the MTA's Red Line into Boston.

Linda, "So James tells me you're an English major. Do you like Dylan?"

Steve, "Do you mean the poet or the singer?"

So right there I pretty much killed my chances for a successful evening, If I had a brain in my head, I should have assumed she meant Bob Dylan, not Dylan Thomas. The rest of the evening our conversation was rather cool and painfully formal, but the ice broke briefly about half way through *My Fair Lady* when Eliza at Ascot screams at the horse she bet on, "Move your bloody arse!" Linda and I looked at each other in surprise, and started to laugh out loud, along with the rest of the audience. How would I rate my first date as a Harvard student? I'd give it a solid 3 ½ — and I probably didn't score that high on her card.

I did not know it at the time, but I was among the first beneficiaries of a class revolution from privilege to meritocracy transforming Harvard College. Only years later when I read the chapter in David Brooks' *Bobos in Paradise* did I understand the historical context. As Brooks explains, in the late fifties and early sixties, two Boston bluebloods, Harvard President James Conant, and the head of the Education Testing Service (ETS), Henry Chauncey, devised standardized tests to help Harvard change from an aristocracy into a meritocracy.

Ironically, a recent major study by William Hiss titled *Defining Promise* indicates that today the Scholastic Aptitude Tests (SAT) may limit diversity by discouraging low SES students from applying to college if their SAT scores are low, even if their grades, a better predictor of success, are high. Hiss' study concludes that "test-optional admissions improves diversity and does not undermine academic quality." Hiss says it's probably not so surprising that a pattern of hard work, discipline and curiosity in high school shows up "as highly predictive, in contrast to what a student does in three or four hours on a particular Saturday morning in a testing room." Some consider the Hiss study a potential game-changer that may prompt schools to evaluate whether there is sufficient value in requiring standardized tests.

You might think that inserting Midwestern country boys into the mix of New England preppies would create cultural conflict. If so, I was not aware of any of it. Harvard was promoting diversity, and the mix was stimulating as we met classmates with plenty of it. But we were all in the same boat trying to survive and hopefully excel at Harvard. Until you had a conversation with a classmate, there was little to distinguish most of us since the dress was almost uniformly downscale, usually jeans or chinos. The Union's dress code required a coat and tie for meals. This requirement was met in the most minimal way, as sports coats would be worn over grubby jeans or chinos. Many ties showed evidence of past meals. The ties would be folded and put back into the coat pocket for next use.

Of course cultural and social-economic differences surfaced during conversations when dialect gave clear indications of origin like Professor Higgins' dialect meter in *My Fair Lady*. Obviously, those of us who worked a term-time job were not preppies or from wealthy families. But I think respect was given on the assumption that you must be OK if Harvard had included you among the chosen. Also, most of us were too self-centered and busy trying to survive and excel at Harvard to worry much about our classmates. Sure we competed for grades, but this was an anonymous undertaking since it was rare to find a friend who shared more than one course among Harvard's extensive curriculum.

The larger distinction that reflected, but also cut across socioeconomic differences, I think, was whether you saw your Harvard experience as a good way to socialize and make contacts for the future, or to focus on grades to the relative exclusion of maximizing contacts. The classic distinction was between the players and the grinds. I was clearly in the latter category, but in my junior year was invited to join one of the Harvard fraternities. I was surprised by the invitation since I was not seeking same, and viewed these private clubs as the exclusive resort of the privileged. I replied with thanks, but explained I could not join the club because I was already too busy with my studies and basketball. This was a true statement, but even if I had a desire to join the club, there was no way I could afford the various dues and other expenses that club life necessitated. I was at Harvard not to cultivate friendships for the future, although I think everyone recognized that contacts were more important than grades. But I got into Harvard on the basis of merit, and the meritocracy would be my ticket via academics. This never was an easy course for me, especially my freshman year.

I probably could have capitalized on a great contact I formed with a wealthy Harvard alumnus the summer of my senior year. Perhaps the best way to describe John P. Chase is with parallels to Oliver's father in *Love Story*. Like Barrett senior, John P. Chase was a legendary Harvard sports hero, having played hockey for the

American team in a prior generation. He was looking for a Harvard student to be a tutor/companion to his twelve year old son for the summer. He hired me after an interview and a recommendation from the Harvard Athletic Department. I remember the long private driveway through a forest of trees to reach his estate near Manchester-by-the-Sea north of Boston. I gasped when I saw the mansion where I would live during the summer, as it was my first close-up experience with great wealth. I could go on in detail, but what impressed me most was the large pond behind the house, which featured black swans imported from Africa at great expense. I had a great summer tutoring the boy, teaching him how to play tennis, and running on the squeaky sands of Singing Beach almost every day. Since Liz's family had a summerhouse in Manchester close to Singing Beach, it is quite possible we passed each other on the sand although she would have been seven since I was 21. Wow, the age gap would have seemed so much wider at those ages than now.

I remember having a conversation with Mr. Chase about the extravagance of the huge sailboat his parents maintained at great expense when so many Americans across the country were struggling to make ends meet. He treated my naiveté with grace as he explained how important the sailboat was to his parents. Mr. Chase was a smart and kind employer, and I probably could have leveraged the relationship into some position in his investment bank, but I was too proud to exploit this relationship. I did not, as I wanted to make my own way in the world based on my own accomplishments rather than contacts.

Writing this now underscores how naïve I was at the time, and reminds me how I never consulted with friends or a mentor in any of the big decisions in my life. I just thought long and hard about the alternatives and then made a decision, confident that I did not need any help given my newly acquired academic credentials. I am not proud of this; I could have benefited greatly from a mentor and another perspective in many of my life choices. The biggest one was leaving Cambridge where many Harvard graduates knew me and I could have capitalized on that without much self-promotion. Self-promotion was a character flaw in the Michigan where I grew up.

Bad Break

Halfway through the freshman basketball season, the unthinkable happened. Some nut case undercut me on a fast break lay-up and I crashed to the floor. In a split second my left leg was broken and my basketball career was over, but my academic career was not. I thank Harvard every time I remember the Michigan coach's words, "Sorry son, but if you couldn't play we would have to give the scholarship to someone who could."

I recovered enough to play junior varsity basketball, but not enough to regain my spot on the varsity squad. Sometimes I would go early to an empty gym and shoot baskets. The joy of shooting baskets in a heated building with polished hardwood floors and large glass backboards was liberating and joyful. Often when stuck on an academic problem or term paper block seated behind my desk, the solutions would come easily on the basketball court and I would hurry back to the dorm and finish the paper.

I along with a faithful few still went to every game and cheered the Crimson from the bleachers. Some highlights included Coach Floyd Wilson, known for his passive style of coaching, getting so emotional over a bad call at a Pennsylvania game that he got up off the bench (surprising the faithful few) and threw a towel high into the air where its flight down to the floor was intercepted by a screen cable about fifteen feet above. The fans rose from their seats and gave the coach a standing ovation while the towel fluttered precariously above the embarrassed coach's head.

Another highlight was the Harvard-Princeton game on February 4, 1964. The game was sold out with a rare standing room only crowd packed into the Indoor Athletic Building (IAB); the only penthouse basketball court in the country. They came to see All-American, Bill Bradley, praised by many as the best college basketball player ever, perform his magic. And he did, but his 30 points were not enough as the Crimson had one of those memorable nights when everything went their way; all the way to an 88-80 upset. Skinny Keith Sedlacek scored a career high 31 points, mostly from long range and big Merle McClung equaled Bradley's total of 30. Barry Williams, the only African-American player on the Crimson team, as usual grabbed the lion's share of rebounds to keep Harvard in the game. Princeton would go on to the Final Four a year later on the strength of Bradley's incomparable talent. But February 4, 1964 was the Crimson's night and gave Harvard basketball fans a taste of what its future could and would be. I went back to my dorm room both elated and dejected, crying myself to sleep over the bad breaks that kept me from being part of the team that night.

amistad

I

With thunder roar the lion tore
Through Cinque's dreams of years before.
With razor fang the monster sprang,
Startled child screams through darkness rang.
Naked Cinque gropes for hunting spear,
Nothing near, but rock, he flings in fear.
What luck or spirits then were there
That struck the beast and killed the terror?

Soon legend grew more than Cinque knew.
He said no, but no words would do.
What celebration followed there,
Dancing, drinking and much fanfare.
So brave had he faced fierce lion down
With bare hands strangled beast, saved the town.
Crowned him chief of all tribe gathered there,
All glory and goods for his welfare.

II

With thunder roar the slavers tore
Through Cinque's hut just like before.
His spear was near but net bound tight
Despite his might, he lost the fight.
Thrown in big boat with cross mast sail,
Chained in dark stench iron clad jail.
Rough seas tossed ship to where couldn't tell,
White demons, sailed screaming into hell.

Warriors look to brave chief once more
With bare hands to kill monster as before.
Poor Cinque knew he no hero true.
Confessed luck, not he, the lion slew.
The shame of nothing he could do
Seemed worse than hell he was sailing to.
Death seemed to him like freedom now.
Ancestors, pray come and help somehow.

Cinque then knew what he must do.
Broke chains, with bare hands white slavers slew.
Then legend grew more than Cinque knew.
He just did what he had to do
To get home and be with family,
But now praised for his divinity.
Not only had he saved the town,
With bare hands had brought slavery down.

III
With thunder roar the terror tore
Through night as for Cinque years before.
Insecure in needless fear, the dark so scary,
The task so large, and we so ordinary.
Whatever you now do: judge or juror,
Banker or bum, driver or doctor,
Carpenter or clerk, peasant or king,
Whatever your role, just do your thing.

Do what you can, help your fellow man,
You never know the most that you can.
Cinque's power is there for you too.
And if it should ever happen to you,
Face your fear and take your stand,
Write your book, extend your hand.
Help a child, sing your song,
Don't be afraid, you will be strong.

Don't worry about why. We don't know
If it's luck or God makes some glow,
Or spirits, or some random fate.
We will never solve this debate.
To your real self always be true,
But then let the power flow through you.
Let the hero come out in you.
Then there is nothing you can not do.

Partners in Justice, by author

Chapter 16
PAINTING

Could it be?

(C)ould it be, Steve wondered, could it just possibly be? For the hundredth time in the last week he held a big heavy art book as close as he could to the oil painting in front of him to determine if there was a match. The book was so heavy that Steve could only hold it up for a few minutes before his arms gave out and he was forced to put the book down. The book was one of the large, lavish art books published by Harry N. Abrams, Inc. in New York City. One of Steve's sub-specialties in his book collecting was Abrams books because he loved these reasonably priced, beautifully executed art books and now he had over forty of them.

One reason for this mini-collection of Abrams art books was his desire to learn more about fine art. Steve had always loved art in high school and managed to work an art class into his schedule. As a break from his studies he loved to draw and especially enjoyed the homework assignments which usually were to draw some specific item like a basketball player grabbing a rebound, a pheasant in field or yes, and I'm not kidding, a pickerel (pike). See "Gender Gap" on page 22, "Partners in Justice" on the facing page and "Players" on page 192. (These one dimensional acrylic paintings are reproduced as evidence of Steve's artistic inclinations and as explanation for his decorative books specialty as discussed in Volume 2 of *Metaphors*, and just because he still likes them.) But his art teacher, Mr. Fuller, was more of a talented craftsman than a connoisseur of fine art. This was evident from one of his proudest possessions – a large wooden storage box strapped to the top of his station wagon. The box was tailored to fit the station wagon and carefully painted on each side length with a colorful pickerel. The box was designed to store Mr. Fuller's fishing gear as fishing was his great escape from the frustration of teaching art to indifferent kids who had elected the art option only because it was known as an easy course. Mr. Fuller could be identified a block away as the flying pike moved about the small Michigan town's quiet streets. Clearly there was a limit to what he could learn from Mr. Fuller.

"Focus Steve, focus," Steve said to himself. How could his mind wander off to pickerels when he had been trying to remember the second reason for his Abrams art books? Oh yes, the second reason was that Steve's room in Kirkland House (known for its concentration of jocks and musicians) shared the same entry as Bob's. Bob was the son of Harry N. Abrams, the name listed as the publisher of those art books. Steve and Bob knew each other as they often said hello passing on the staircase. But Bob would usually sit with his sophomore friends in the Kirkland House dining room and Steve usually sat with a changing group of seniors. After Harvard, Bob had joined his father in art book publishing and later started his own company, Abbeville Press. Among the Abbeville Press books in his library, Steve has a copy of *Modern Art at Harvard* that Bob gave to all classmates on their 25th reunion. What fascinating stories he must have about the inside world of art book publishing. Perhaps I should try to have lunch with Bob the next time I'm in New York City, Steve thought as his mind wandered once again from the comparison of book and painting in front of him. And oh yes, the other point was that Steve had not been able to schedule Harvard's popular introductory art course Fine Arts 13. Some other course required for his English major always blocked the way. Had he been able to take Fine Arts

13, perhaps he would have the more sophisticated taste that would enable him to better evaluate the oil painting in front of him.

Could it be? Steve asked himself for the one hundredth and one time. Sure the odds were a million to one against it, but still better than the lottery; and *Antiques Roadshow* often interviewed the lucky few who had beat the odds by finding a valuable painting hidden in the attic. Maybe, just maybe, my ship has come in, Steve thought. The metaphor triggered another round of distracted thought as Steve chuckled realizing that he had adopted Barry Williams' favorite phrase. Steve had met Barry after a Harvard basketball game shortly after Steve had broken his leg. When they later overlapped to co-write a term paper for Archibald Cox's Constitutional Law class, Steve had gotten to know Barry better. "What's up, Barry?" Barry's frequent response was some variation of "Things looking up. I think my ship's about to come in." Of course the metaphor meant his life was about to change after some big score that would make him rich.

Steve had always felt sorry for Barry because the big, black bruiser did the tough overlooked work of grabbing the lion's share of rebounds while McClung and Sedlacek got most of the publicity. "McClung matches Bradley's 30 and Sedlacek 31 in stunning upset of Princeton" the *Crimson* headline screamed the next morning in the first *Crimson* front page story anyone remembered for a Harvard basketball team. Nowhere in this account were Barry's twelve key rebounds mentioned. Barry once confided in Steve that coach Wilson had forced him to shave off his moustache if he wanted to play for Harvard and Barry had resented what he believed to be his prejudiced white coach ever since.

"Focus, Steve, focus," Steve told himself once again. Your mind keeps wandering through old memories when you need it for the task at hand. "Could it be that my ship has finally come in?"

Note: Because I have a premonition that the Grim Reaper will soon be knocking on my door, I have not taken the time necessary to separate the wheat from the chaff. Two more volumes will be necessary to complete *Metaphors: A Reverse Love Story.* This "excuse" reminds me of Blaise Pascal's comment in a letter to a friend, "I have made this a rather long letter because I haven't had the time to make it short."

Players, by author

Metaphors Vol. 1
INDEX OF POEMS

Metaphors Vol. 1
INDEX OF PHOTOS

DON'T STOP NOW!

Order
Metaphors Vol 1: A Reverse Love Story
for Kindle

at Amazon.com

Metaphors Vol 2: Serendipitous Collecting
is coming soon.

Email the author at
ConceptsUnlimited@estreet.com

Author's Main Floor Library

Made in the USA
Charleston, SC
23 June 2014